ZAMZAM

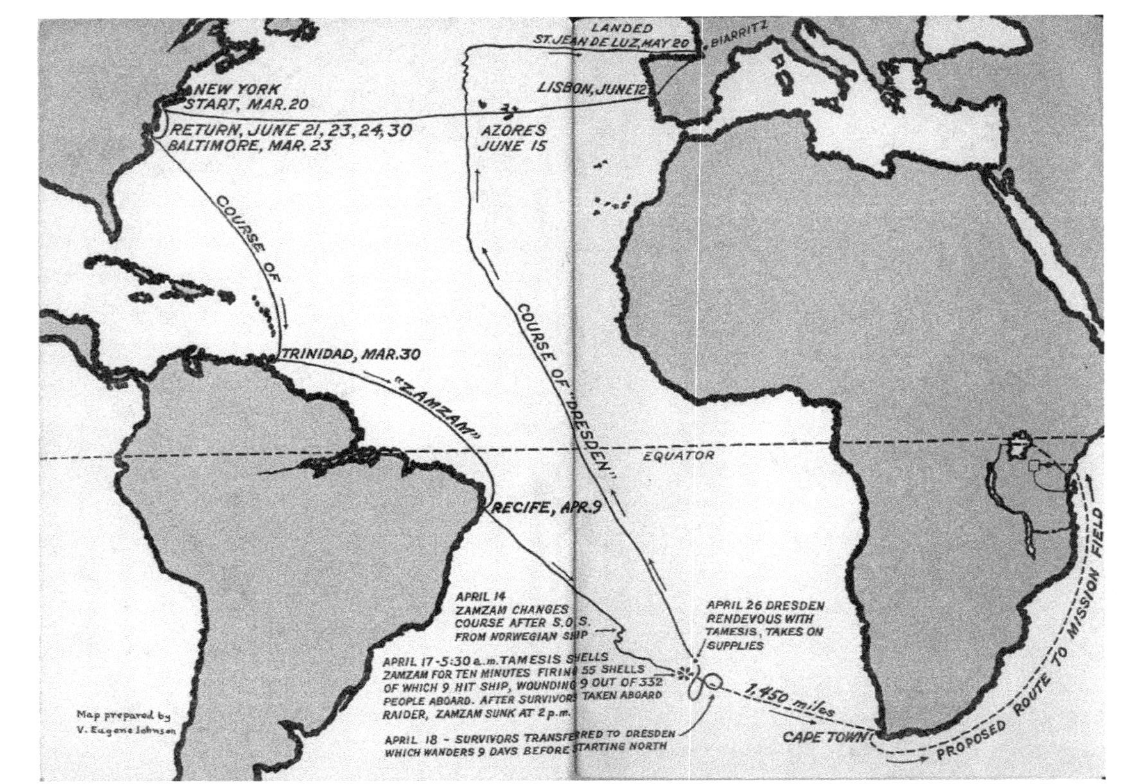

NEW YORK
START, MAR. 20
RETURN, JUNE 21, 23, 24, 30
BALTIMORE, MAR. 23
COURSE OF
TRINIDAD, MAR. 30
"ZAMZAM"
RECIFE, APR. 9
LANDED
ST. JEAN DE LUZ, MAY 20
BIARRITZ
LISBON, JUNE 12
AZORES
JUNE 15
COURSE OF "DRESDEN"
EQUATOR
APRIL 14
ZAMZAM CHANGES
COURSE AFTER S.O.S.
FROM NORWEGIAN SHIP
APRIL 17 - 5:30 a.m. TAMESIS SHELLS
ZAMZAM FOR TEN MINUTES FIRING 55 SHELLS
OF WHICH 9 HIT SHIP, WOUNDING 9 OUT OF 332
PEOPLE ABOARD. AFTER SURVIVORS TAKEN ABOARD
RAIDER, ZAMZAM SUNK AT 2 p.m.
APRIL 18 - SURVIVORS TRANSFERRED TO DRESDEN
WHICH WANDERS 9 DAYS BEFORE STARTING NORTH
APRIL 26 DRESDEN
RENDEVOUS WITH
TAMESIS, TAKES ON
SUPPLIES
1,450 miles
CAPE TOWN
PROPOSED ROUTE TO MISSION FIELD
Map prepared by
V. Eugene Johnson

ZAMZAM

The Story of a Strange Missionary Odyssey

By
The Augustana Synod Passengers

Edited by
S. Hjalmar Swanson, D.D.

Quiet Waters Publications
Bolivar, Missouri
2007

For information contact:

Quiet Waters Publications
P.O. Box 34, Bolivar, MO 65613-0034.
E-mail: QWP@usa.net.

For prices and order information visit:

http://www.quietwaterspub.com

ISBN 1-931475-35-0
ISBN 978-1-931475-35-8

ZAMZAM

The Story of a Strange Missionary Odyssey

By

THE AUGUSTANA SYNOD PASSENGERS

Edited by

S. HJALMAR SWANSON, D.D.

1941
MINNEAPOLIS, MINNESOTA
THE BOARD OF FOREIGN MISSIONS
OF THE AUGUSTANA SYNOD

PRINTED IN U·S·A·

Second Printing, December, 1941

AUGUSTANA BOOK CONCERN
Printers and Binders
ROCK ISLAND, ILLINOIS
1941

CONTENTS

Zamzam passengers and crew climbing down rope ladder into lifeboat on starboard side. Photo by *Life* magazine.

A MISSIONARY SHIP

THE EDITOR

And embarking in a ship . . . which was about to sail . . . we put to sea. Acts 27. 2.

The *S. S. Zamzam* left New York (Hoboken), March 20, 1941, for Suez, via Trinidad, Pernambuco, Capetown, and Mombasa. It was declared a neutral ship. Its passengers were chiefly missionaries bound for Africa.

Its American agents wrote us January 10: "The *Zamzam*, formerly the *S. S. Leicestershire* of the Bibby Line, is now one of the passenger liners of the Egyptian Government fleet, and flies the Egyptian flag. She is therefore a neutral vessel. This line is now maintaining a regular service of passenger and freight ships . . . avoiding the so-called 'combat zones.' . . . To date we have booked more than 120 missionaries and their families."

Shortly after her departure the agents gave us the following information: "The *Zamzam* sailed at 10:55 P.M., March 20, with 201 passengers. We are pleased to announce that 144 of these were missionaries, of whom 33 were children under fourteen years of age."

Twenty Protestant denominations as well as the Roman Catholic Church were represented among its passengers of missionaries. These missionaries were bound for thirteen different areas or provinces in Africa. Probably never before had a ship left our shores for the "Dark Continent" with such a host of Christian ambassadors.

The Augustana Synod had the following members among its passengers:

Mrs. Elmer R. Danielson and children, Laurence, Eleanor, Evelyn, Luella, Wilfred, and Lois;

Rev. Ralph D. Hult;

Rev. and Mrs. V. Eugene Johnson and children, Victor and David;

Miss Velura Kinnan;

Dr. and Mrs. C. Einar Norberg and children, Marie J., Carl E., and Ruth E.;

Miss Esther M. Olson.

It is no easy matter to cross the oceans now. There are so many things which must be considered, things we hardly dreamed of a few years ago.

Few are the boats which now carry passengers to Africa or Asia, and ships flying our own flag are not always available. Generally the few ships which sail have their reservations filled six months or more in advance.

Then there is the more than ever important American passport which must be obtained from our State Department, and when this has been secured it must receive a visa from the British consul, if one is to enter a British-mandated possession such as Tanganyika. This visa, under present rules brought about by the great war, can not be received until the government at the port of entry, Tanganyika, has officially informed the British consul in America that the person in question is acceptable over there. To make all these arrangements by mail under present conditions may take half a year. It therefore becomes necessary, occasionally, to resort to cables, and when it came to making the necessary arrangements for our *Zamzam* passengers, the cables saved months of time. It was only two or three days before the boat left that we were assured of the required papers for all our passengers, and had the sailing date not been deferred Mrs. Danielson and family would not have been aboard.

Mrs. Danielson had the shortest time in which to get

ready, and we marveled at the fact that she was in New York City ready to go aboard when the ship set sail.

Her husband, Rev. Elmer R. Danielson, volunteered to return to Africa alone in the summer of 1940, since at that time there was a ruling denying women and children entrance to British East Africa. When we received a letter from her husband asking if it might be possible for his family now to come to Africa in company with the other missionaries, we called her by telephone.

"Do you wish to go, and do you think it will be possible for you to get ready, if necessary papers can be obtained?" we asked.

Yes, she would get both herself and her children ready. Most of us would ask for a month or two, at least, in which to prepare for a journey to Africa. She was ready in a week!

But our cabled request for an entry permit waited for an answer. The ship was now scheduled to sail March 15, and on March 11, after consulting the British consul in Chicago, I was forced to telegraph Mrs. Danielson: "No visa obtainable. You must wait."

Next day we were told that sailing had again been deferred until March 19.

Mrs. Danielson suggested trying again. This we did, and through the quick and courteous co-operation of the British consuls in Chicago and New York City, it became possible to wire Mrs. Danielson at Lindsborg, Kansas, on March 14, that her visa was obtainable in New York City. Three days afterwards she was in New York City.

To some it may seem strange to take children of school age on such a journey at this time of the year. But let us remind you that among our missionaries were two experienced school teachers, who were on their way out to Tanganyika to open a school for our missionaries' children. They had school books and necessary material with them on the boat, and the first day out of New York City school started. Other missionaries' children also availed themselves of this opportunity, and this school continued until the shelling of the *Zamzam*, April 17. We feel certain that these children will carry with them lessons for life from these school days on the *Zamzam*.

During their stay in New York City, our missionaries were the guests of the Lutheran Home for Women. Dr. Emmy Evald and her assistants did all in their power to make their last hours in America pleasant. The memory of such kindness and hospitality lingers with the travelers. A farewell reception was tendered our missionaries at the Bethlehem Lutheran Church, Dr. Gideon Olson, pastor, the evening before embarkation.

Dr. Ralph H. Long, executive secretary of the National Lutheran Council and director of Lutheran World Action, visited with our missionaries as they boarded the boat. Thereupon he wrote us: "There are a great many missionaries on the boat and I sincerely hope the boat will make a safe journey. . . . When I saw the great number of missionaries who were going I thought of a company of soldiers going forth without the visible presence of a captain, without any mounted guns for defense, and yet one which will probably accomplish for the Lord and for the world more than many of the finely disciplined armies that are on the march today."

The ship was, after several delays, supposed to sail March 19. It did not leave the harbor, however, until late the following evening. Aboard the ship Dr. Norberg penned his impressions the next morning.

"At last," he wrote, "we hear the old familiar chug! chug! of the propeller and engine, and we are heading south. We finally got started late last night, and it was a most unusual departure from this mighty metropolis. As we slowly slid down the Hudson River past the brilliantly illumined Statue of Liberty a large group of missionaries on board gathered on deck and sang a few hymns, such as, 'He Leadeth Me, O Blessed Thought,' 'Send Out Thy Light,' and many others. With the millions of lights from fantastic Manhattan, Staten Island, Jersey City, and other places of the surrounding country, including the lit torch held high by the Statue of Liberty lighting our way out of the harbor, I could not help but reflect upon the fact that few are the harbors today where so much light is permitted at night. May God in His infinite mercy grant that America's harbors may ever be lit and keep on sending out many more boatloads of missionaries to countries where God's gospel is yet unknown."

"The children's school is in full swing every day," he wrote in another letter. "All the children of school age are attending. I certainly feel that we are signally blessed to have those two girls with us as teachers. We are close to 150 missionaries on this ship, of whom about twenty are Roman Catholics and the rest are from various Protestant denominations in America. Is it not reassuring to know that the American churches can send so many missionaries off to Africa? For every missionary on this ship there are hundreds of Christians at home who are with us in prayers and gifts, that His kingdom may be extended to far-off Africa."

Could anything happen to such a ship? If so, did God not hear our prayers?

God has not promised to keep His children out of trials, but He has promised to be with them in their troubles. "Fear not, for I have redeemed thee. When thou passest through the waters, I will be with thee."—Isaiah 43. 2. He who accompanied the three young men into the midst of the burning fiery furnace (Daniel 3), and Daniel when cast among the lions, and Paul when in prison and shipwreck, also accompanied our missionaries on the *Zamzam*. In the darkest hour of their terrific experience He went as far as to spread His rainbow in the western sky. Had He visually appeared on the waters, He could hardly have said more than to point them to His promises. Now He spoke to them in a language that Christians of every tongue could understand. Our prayers were heard and answered. Every life was saved by the grace of God, who still is found to work miracles. What His purpose was in permitting them to pass through these trials may not yet be evident to us, but we believe that even this was intended to glorify His name.

When our missionaries were safely aboard the *Zamzam*, March 20, we felt relieved, because we knew, after many efforts, that at last they were on their way to the many black folks in Tanganyika who needed the gospel and their healing ministry so badly. Yet we felt an anxious concern over their safety. Each day thousands of us here in the homeland, as well as the missionaries across the seas, prayed and waited, glad for each day that passed, knowing that it was bringing them nearer to their destination.

"We will send you a cable as soon as we land," they had promised. Now it was time that this cable should come. Many of us began to wonder.

"I'm wondering if you have heard anything from our Africa-bound missionary party?" wrote Mrs. Hult May 2. As we came into the middle of May many others began to ask the same question.

The Board of Foreign Missions met May 15.

One guess made on that day came nearer the truth than we realized. "Maybe they are not permitted to send a cable," it was suggested. We hoped then that they were in Mombasa. Five days later they landed in France.

MAY NINETEENTH

THE EDITOR

They that sow in tears shall reap in joy.
Psalm 126. 5.

May 19, 1941 is the saddest day in Augustana Synod history. We praise God that He turned what this day seemed like a crushing blow, followed by a dark night, into an occasion of rejoicing so soon.

How merciful God was to the first disciples when He let Easter come so soon after Good Friday!

We might easily have been kept in uncertainty or despair for weeks. Now it was only for 24 hours.

My telephone rang early on the morning of May 19. I was hoping that it was Western Union with a cable from Africa. Instead it was my secretary asking with a quivering voice, "Have you heard that there was a radio announcement that the *Zamzam* is lost?"

Most of that morning was spent at the telephone. The newspapers and press services not only asked us for all information available, but they also co-operated most kindly by instantly telephoning us every bit of news or conjecture about the *Zamzam* and its passengers the minute it was received. We also made contact with the nearest relatives of our missionaries. Thousands in our Synod, from coast to coast, were deeply affected. From many parts of our land I have heard them say: "I could not work that day!" Our nineteen who had set out so joyously in the Lord for the great African harvest fields were dead.

In company with Dr. Leonard Kendall we went to call upon the mother of Pastor V. Eugene Johnson. But how were we to comfort her?

She bore up bravely, probably not realizing yet to the full the import of it all, while we visited with her. The emotional reaction probably came afterward. We could only point to God's promises and pray together, and then suggest that there might still be hope. "In the South Atlantic it would be more likely that they had been attacked by a raider than by a submarine. We have heard of raiders saving the passengers when they sink a ship. Let us wait for further reports. There is yet a possibility that they are alive." This was the best that we could hope for and say, because our fears were stronger than our faith.

We meant to comfort Doris and Daniel Johnson, but they had greater faith than we. They had assurance in their souls that all would turn out well. I could only pray: "God, let not their faith be put to shame!"

In the afternoon the Executive Committee of the Board of Foreign Missions came together to pray, to weep, and to consult about any steps that might be taken to obtain official information. We contacted Congressman Oscar Youngdahl in Washington, and he promised to secure for us from the Department of State any information which might be in its possession about the *Zamzam* sinking and the fate of its passengers. This he did immediately and sent us several valuable communications on following days.

The teachers and students of our church schools were all concerned. From the dean of the Seminary came this telegram: "If this hour be the Gethsemane in the history of our Synod's foreign mission, then we of the Seminary would join with you in asking God to give us grace to utter the difficult petition, 'Thy will be done.' Surely the Lord is not going to let His great cause suffer defeat. We are praying that what may appear as a defeat now shall ultimately result in a greater victory for the mission cause in our Synod. As for His messengers on the *Zamzam*, they are in God's keeping and we hope to see them again whether that be down here or up yonder."

When night came it was hard to sleep.

Then dawned a new day with Easter joy. Before I was out of bed the telephone rang.

"This is the United Press," said the voice at the other end of the line. "We just received some good news about your friends. They are all alive and safe." And then he added: "Have you anything to say?"

"Thank God! is all that I can say. It seems too good to be true."

We had been walking in the dark valley with our friends. Now we were suddenly taken to the very mountaintop with God. It was a real Easter experience. We could now better understand what we read about the first disciples, "They still disbelieved for joy."

As the hours of this day sped on, the radio and the press continued to give reports to the effect that all the passengers were safe and were being brought to some neutral port. We were also thinking of our missionaries in Africa, particularly Pastors Danielson and Olson. Had the news broken over there? We had no way of knowing what agonies they might be passing through. We cabled Dr. Geo. N. Anderson, president of our Africa mission: "Reports *Zamzam* sunk. All passengers safe at German-occupied port." This was sent May 20. Apparently it took some days before it was delivered to our missionaries in Tanganyika.

The same day Congressman Youngdahl wired: "State Department has not yet received official confirmation of rescue of all persons aboard *Zamzam.* Cable being sent today to Germany officially to verify radio reports."

May 22 he sent us another message: "State Department advised they received telegram from American consul Bordeaux advising all American passengers safe at St. Jean de Luz, France, and that he is proceeding to St. Jean to determine communications available."

We now knew that all our missionaries had been saved, but as yet we could only guess as to the experiences which they had passed through. As yet they were not in position to communicate with us while they continued to be the "guests" of the German government.

Efforts were made through the Foreign Missions Conference of North America and in other ways to ascertain if the missionaries would be permitted to proceed to Africa. Over in France our missionaries, as we later ascertained, made similar inquiries. May 29 we received this message from Hon. Cordell Hull, Secretary of State: "Your telegram of May 27 received regarding your missionaries from *S. S. Zamzam* proceed Africa. As route of travel from Portugal to Africa is through combat zone area waters, permission to validate passports for such purpose can not be granted. Information received from Department's representatives abroad indicates Americans from *Zamzam* safe and well, comfortably accomodated at Biarritz where they are given freedom of city pending release for travel. Department's representatives in touch with them and are looking after their welfare."

Then reports came that all missionaries who could prove American citizenship would be released and taken through Spain to Lisbon, Portugal, from which port they would be assisted aboard the earliest boats possible for return to America. As soon as our missionaries reached Sintra, near Lisbon, June 3, they sent us the following cable: "Isaiah 63. 9. All well. Greet friends and relatives. Washington orders us home. Psalm 124. Your Nineteen. Norberg."

How happy we were to receive this cable! It was the first direct word from our missionaries since the day their ship sailed from Pernambuco, South America. It was received June 4. They were all not only saved, but also well!

We opened our Bibles and read Psalm 124:

"If it had not been Jehovah who was on our side,
Let Israel now say,
If it had not been Jehovah who was on our side,
When men rose up against us;
Then they had swallowed us up alive,
When their wrath was kindled against us:
Then the waters had overwhelmed us,
The stream had gone over our soul;
Then the proud waters had gone over our soul.
Blessed be Jehovah, who hath not given us as a prey to their teeth.
Our soul is escaped as a bird out of the snare of the fowlers:
The snare is broken, and we are escaped.
Our help is in the name of Jehovah,
Who made heaven and earth."

From Sintra it also was possible for our missionaries to write letters to friends and relatives in America and in Africa. These were the first letters they had been able to send since leaving Pernambuco, about two months earlier. How much they had lived through since then! They had much to write about, but what their thousands of friends were most anxious to hear now was that they were well and had suffered no harm from their strange experiences.

Then came reports that the *Zamzam* survivors were being placed on ships bound for America. From the State Department came a telegram June 16: "Reference your telegram of June 13 concerning probable date arrival New York of *Zamzam* survivors. Velura Kinnan and Esther

Olson scheduled arrive Portuguese steamer *Mouzinho* June 22. V. Eugene Johnson and Carl E. Norberg and their families scheduled arrive Portuguese steamer *Serpa Pinto* June 24. Cordell Hull."

Saturday morning, June 21, I arrived at the Lutheran Home in New York. Just as I came through the door Mrs. Carlson, Dr. Evald's daughter, was at the telephone. She was asking somebody when the *S. S. Mouzinho* would arrive, and I heard her say, "Is it docking now?" Yes, although it was due on Sunday it was docking in the harbor now, and in a few minutes the passengers would begin to disembark.

Mrs. Carlson was kind enough to accompany me to Pier 7, Staten Island. It took a long hour to get there by subway and ferry and bus. I managed to get near to the foot of the gangplank but could obtain no information regarding our passengers. For some hours I stood there watching the passengers, mostly Jewish refugees, come ashore. It was a study in human emotions. Many of these refugees were children whose parents were dead or in concentration camps. Some were old and tottering. Many had escaped living deaths. Now they were in America! Some of the folks at the pier became uncontrollable when they recognized an aged parent or some other relative on the deck. They called at the top of their voices only to have their cries drowned by a hundred other voices. They stormed the gangplank repeatedly, and some had to be forcibly led away by the guards. The men embraced one another and kissed fervently. It was apparent that Jewish folks are very emotional. Had we known what fears and sufferings and tragedies had intervened since some of these folks last met, we would have appreciated their released emotional frenzy much better. But we understood in part. After all, were we not there to meet friends over whom we but a few weeks

(1) Mrs. Elmer R. Danielson and children. Photo by PM Syndicate. (2) Miss Velura Kinnan and Miss Esther Olson. (3) Rev. Ralph D. Hult.

ago had wept as dead? It was a setting in which we felt at home.

Our two missionaries had been among the first to disembark, and having very little baggage they had slipped through customs before our arrival. We had the joy of meeting them a little later at the Lutheran Home. Out of the depths they had returned to America and the Augustana Synod. Yet they looked both well and happy. Now they had to tell us as much as possible about what our missionaries had passed through. That evening we had the first thanksgiving service, at the Home.

Monday morning, June 23, I was off to Staten Island again to meet the *Serpa Pinto.* It was another Portuguese ship, carrying another overcrowded load of Jewish refugees, among whom some *Zamzam* survivors had been pushed in after every accomodation had been more than sold out. Boats like these must make good money for their owners as long as they manage to stay afloat.

Yes, here they were, hale and happy: Dr. and Mrs. C. Einar Norberg and their three children, and Rev. and Mrs. V. Eugene Johnson and their two youngest children. Another Easter experience! Soon we were on our way to the Lutheran Home, where eleven of our survivors were now comfortably housed.

Next day, June 24, the *S. S. Exeter* was due with Mrs. Elmer R. Danielson and her children. It was to dock at one o'clock, but by this time we had discovered that this might also mean eleven or twelve o'clock or anytime in the afternoon. Consequently Dr. Norberg and I were off in the forenoon for Hoboken and the pier. The boat docked at three o'clock. It did not take long until we could see Mrs. Danielson on deck. What a thrill it was! How you all would have enjoyed being there when she came down the gankplank surrounded by her six children who clung closely to her. I could only wish that her husband might have been there to greet this plucky and brave missionary mother just then. His brother was there instead. He had come from Meriden, Connecticut, to take the Danielson family up there for a few days of rest and family rejoicing.

When the reporters and photographers and customs officials were through with Mrs. Danielson we said good-by to her near the pier, as she was sped on her way to Meriden. As they moved out of our sight we again thanked God for their safety. Two months ago these children had been adrift in the South Atlantic. Had even one been lost, how different this homecoming would have been! "Bless the Lord, O my soul, and forget not all His benefits!"

Now we had seen and greeted eighteen of our missionary group. Rev. Ralph D. Hult had not returned. With much relief we read a telegram from the Department of State stating that he was aboard the *S. S. Excalibur* and would arrive in New York June 30.

Now began a unique series of receptions and thanksgiving services.

The first one was at the Bethlehem Church in Brooklyn, Dr. Gideon Olson, pastor. A little more than three months earlier, as already mentioned, a farewell reception had been tendered in this church for this group. Now warm words of welcome home were spoken. Most of our pastors in the great metropolitan area were present. The missionaries related some of their experiences, and together we praised a merciful God.

That same evening we boarded a train for Jamestown, N. Y., the whole missionary party except Mrs. Danielson and children, and of course Rev. Hult.

We arrived in Jamestown at noon the next day. A large group of friends had assembled on the platform. As we emerged from the train they were singing, "Praise God from whom all blessings flow!" Pastor Constant Johnson, I was told, had arranged this and was going to be the song leader, but when he saw the once-mourned-as-dead missionaries something came into his throat and eyes, "which made him a very poor song leader." The others, struggling with their tears of joy, managed to go through with the beautiful greeting. It was another impressive, unforgettable moment. Thank God for Christian fellowship!

In the evening we assembled in the beautifully redecorated sanctuary of the First Lutheran Church. Words of welcome were spoken by the pastor and by Dr. Felix Hanson, president of the New York Conference. The missionaries spoke. Here, as in the other places, fitting and beautiful music was rendered, and we praised God for His deliverance. This was Miss Esther Olson's home city and she had therefore the joy of spending a few hours with her parents.

Early Thursday morning we were on our way again, bound for Chicago, and when we pulled into the Dearborn Station we were immediately met by Rev. Theodore L. Rydbeck and some of his members. Another happy reunion, and then we were whisked to homes for supper and then to the Messiah Church.

Here we were greeted by a packed church and with tender words of welcome. A large number of our pastors were in the audience. Everyone in the congregation was touched by the stories of God's miraculous mercy as told by our missionaries.

Next day we were on our way again, now for Minneapolis, all except Mrs. Norberg and her children, who felt the tugging at the heartstrings of the dear ones in Nebraska and therefore left from Chicago for Omaha.

What a joyous meeting and reunion at the Milwaukee Station in Minneapolis! Grandma Johnson, Doris and

Daniel Johnson were there, and a host of other relatives and friends. Between reunion joys and reporters and photographers Dr. Leonard Kendall had reason to feel concerned over how to get us all on our way to the Messiah Church, where a capacity congregation was anxiously waiting to see and to hear our survivors.

This service constituted what might be called the official homecoming and thanksgiving service, because here they were greeted by, among others, Dr. P. O. Bersell, the president of Augustana Synod, and Mrs. Daniel T. Martin, the president of the Woman's Missionary Society of the Synod.

Sunday evening, June 29, a similar service was held in the Gustavus Adolphus Church, St. Paul, Rev. C. Vernon Swenson, pastor. This service was sponsored by the District Woman's Missionary Society and the churches of the St. Paul District.

* * *

What experiences did our missionaries pass through, and how did God intervene to save their lives and bring them safely back from shelling and from drowning and from prison?

We have asked each one to tell one phase of their experiences.

Here you will have this in their own words.

ON THE "ZAMZAM"

MRS. ELMER R. DANIELSON

They that go down to the sea in ships,
These see the works of Jehovah.
Psalm 107. 23–24.

What a thrill! Homeward bound for Africa. My heart beat just a little faster as I remembered the African friends whom it has been our great joy to see translated from darkness into His marvelous light. Even our little ones were all anticipation as they exclaimed: "Daddy will meet us in Africa." With me, it was the "bridegroom" awaiting at home for me, and no traveling on a vast sea could efface my hope of that happy reunion. How like *life* itself!

There was so much hymn singing on the pier by friends of embarking passengers that already I felt it was going to be a "missionary pilgrimage" to Africa. Out of the 200 passengers there were some 120 Protestant missionaries, besides the 20 Roman Catholic fathers who also were going to their mission work. Never before had I traveled with so many workers going to Africa, not for the gold that glitters, but to seek gems for His diadem.

We said good-by to friends and went inside to see what our "home" for the next two months would be like. This Egyptian boat was thirty-one years old, and was an 8,300-ton ship. I have never found a smoother riding vessel, nor have I seen cleaner decks. During the voyage the inside walls were cleaned, some renovations were made, and painting was done. Despite some things which were not so commendable for the ship, I like to remember those things which endeared the ship even to us. The Egyptians were proud of her. Had she not carried many Mohammedans on sacred pilgrimages to Mecca? Had she not carried British troops during the World War? Surely nothing could ever happen to their sacred ship.

Maybe it would be well to give you a resume of the type of passengers aboard, bound for Africa, a conglomeration of nationalities and vocations which was bound to make for cliques, be they social or otherwise. Out of the 202 passengers, there were 73 women and 35 children. There was a mixed group of 138 Americans, 26 Canadians, 25 Britishers, five South Africans, four Belgians, one Italian, one Norwegian, and two Greeks. Of the 129 members of the crew only the captain and the chief engineer were British, 106 were Egyptian, nine were Sudanese, two Yugoslav, one Czech, six Greek, one French, and two Turk. There was a banding together because of nationalistic lines as well as work. As the days passed we found these distinct cliques on board: the Catholic fathers, the six tobacco buyers from North Carolina, the 24 ambulance boys, the 120 missionaries, and then the Egyptian crew, as well as those passengers who belonged to neither of the above groups.

Night came the first day and we were still in port. How we had hurried to get to the boat in time, and here we still were! It was not until the evening of March 20 that the chief purser came along and happily announced: "Here I have the permit to sail. *Now* we can go." The engines were throbbing, and everything was ready. In another half hour we actually steamed out of harbor. Groups were singing on the deck, as we glided by the majestic Statue of Liberty. She held high the lighted torch in her hand, the lighted crown shone brightly in the night. It was a beautiful sight in the still eventide, saying good-by to America for another four and a half years' term of service. Oh, that farewell look at the Statue of Liberty, the last thing one sees as he glides out of the harbor, and it is the first to greet the wanderer on his return. Now we retired for the night, thanking God for the privilege of again going to garner sheaves in Africa, and praying His journeying mercies on the trip just begun.

Life on the *Zamzam* soon took on its routine order. Breakfasts were served from seven-thirty to nine. The children were initiated back into schooldays for two and a half hours each forenoon, Miss Olson taking the upper grades and Miss Kinnan the lower grades. Eyodele, a colored girl, was among the fifteen children attending school. Her parents told me that the name Eyodele means: "Joy has come to our house." I noticed no color prejudice among the children toward this new schoolmate. Were not even they going as missionaries to her people, and had not many of the children been born in Africa, the land of the blacks? Even the smaller children were often kept for kindergarten games and play for an hour by Mrs. Johnson and some of the other mothers.

Then came an interlude each forenoon from 11:30 until 12:15 when those who could would meet to sing and pray together, to read His Word and to testify of His love. There was much praying for the "unsaved" on board, that they too might know Jesus as a Saviour. A violin and trombone added life to the group singing. Thus in a quiet nook of the ship each day this spirit-minded group met, while in the near-by bar room others met for smoking, drinking, card playing, and other worldly amusements.

After dinner each day there was the quiet hour, when many of us mothers felt it necessary to get some needed rest also, while our little ones slept. Keeping an alert watch on six youngsters on a boat with an open railing, open spaces where the life boats stand in readiness, and with no daddy to share it all—well, it is a full-time job, and one often *runs* a good part of the journey to Africa. The more ambitious availed themselves of Ki-Swahili study taught by Rev. V. Eugene Johnson before teatime each day. For many of us there was individual brushing up on Kinilamba and other tribal languages. How we all longed to become better vessels to carry the gospel to those to whom we were going, and the spiritual requisites were not forgotten.

At three-thirty each day the tea bell sounded, and there over the teacup we all found one common bond of sociability. Even the little children acclaimed the factory biscuits a real delicacy. They did not so much enjoy the Egyptian spiced cooking at mealtimes.

Recreation was found in shuffleboard games, rope jumping, checkers, and hobbies of different kinds. With the less active ladies it was embroidery or knitting. Some passengers spent much time in some quiet nook reading. Writing letters to loved ones was not an uncommon occupation, especially a few days before we were to reach the next port.

To add a little variety to the routine, there might be injections for tetanus, whooping cough, or some other preventive measures. Our little children were so fearful of needles by this time, that they feared the kind doctors as well. Some later year they may thank God for these preventions and the doctors who serve.

Life on the *Zamzam* was much the same from day to day. Some succumbed to seasickness when the waves rolled higher, but we had few such days. One of the first uneasy moments for some perhaps came when on March 23 we put in at Baltimore for the day to pick up additional cargo and passengers. Then Captain William Smith, looking down on the pier where 120 missionaries were singing "Jesus Saviour, Pilot Me," with impudent competition from a less reverent group growled: "Bible punchers and sky pilots are bad luck. Mark me!"

From Trinidad, our boat began to travel blacked-out. What a strange new experience for most of us, to find our way in the dark, after supper, to our rooms along an unlighted outer deck, stubbing our toes on deck chairs, and all but falling or bumping into some other person groping in our direction in the dark! What a thrill to arrive at the right cabin finally, to knock on the door and warn the little ones: "Lights off, Mother wants to come in!" Several nights I rejoiced in a moon to help me find the way, and I was kindly rebuked by an old lady: "When you travel blacked-out, thank God not for moonlight nights, but for the blackest ones. Then we are safest." This was different. Was it all because of war? And yet, were we not going to Africa on His mission? One of my daughters often came to me: "Mother, I'm scared the boat will sink. I just *know* it will!" I always tried to calm her with: "We're riding safely. Jesus is our Pilot! Let's trust ourselves to Him." In my heart I knew no fear, but she must have had premonitions of something just ahead.

One awe-inspiring night I will not soon forget. It was around one o'clock and we were sneaking along in the dark. All at once, we were startled from our sleep by one long blast, followed in a few seconds by another. At the third we were up, and hurriedly the life jackets were being secured on each child. Something must be wrong, a boat's whistle when we wished to be unobserved. I stepped outside my cabin door. It was pitch black, misting, water five inches deep near the door. Was our boat sinking? Soon a venerable missionary came sloshing in the water and said: "Don't be alarmed. It is just a fog horn." Those were the sweetest words I had heard on the whole trip. We learned the next day that others had been fearful, too, even though many no doubt laughed at our night drill practice. How I thanked

God the next week when we had to make our hurried exit that we had had our midnight practice.

The last Sunday on the *Zamzam* was a God-sent one. First of all on this glorious Easter morn, the children under the direction of their teachers testified so impressively in song, recitations and drills of the great Easter message: "He is risen! Jesus lives!" Then followed the service for the adults, and the "breaking of bread" together. God knew we needed a special strengthening of soul for that hard week just ahead of us.

As later we sat at the dinner table Rev. Dosumu, colored, felt sad that the next Sunday maybe we would be at Capetown, and it would mean the parting of the ways for many of us. This trip had not been different from others, many new friendships in Jesus had been made for eternity. I must confess that despite the farewells ahead, I was almost impatient to get to Capetown. Oh, for an airmail from "our daddy"! The last letter received was written November 29, and it seemed an age.

As to any scares along the way, only one is of importance. Permit me now to quote from the magazine, *Life*, for June 23. "The first real scare came on the afternoon of April 14. At 3:25 the ship which had been steering southwest swung hard to the west and, at top speed, headed back in the direction of South America. Around six o'clock, as dusk gathered, she veered southwest, holding that course until ten o'clock, when she turned south. It was not until an uneasy dawn revealed an empty sea that she finally squared away again for Capetown. Later the captain told me what had happened. Shortly after three o'clock his radiomen had picked up a conventional British warning, QQQ, meaning "suspicious ship," from a ship that sounded hard by. A few minutes later, while the radiomen were glued to the receivers, a second signal smashed in, a series of R's, meaning Raider, followed by a strident message: 'Being chased by a German raider. Course zero (due north). Fourteen knots.' She flashed her name as the *Tai-Yin*, of Norwegian registry, and her position as Lat. 22° 30′′ S., Long. 16° 10′′ W., which would put her less than twenty miles southeast of where the *Zamzam* turned, just below the horizon, and fleeing directly across her track."

This will give you a picture, no doubt, of the uneasiness of those in charge of the ship and a few others, but for most of us, we knew very little as to why we had turned around, except that something unusual, some suspicious vessel was in the waters somewhere. I noticed very little change in the serious outlook of the passengers. There were some prayer groups here and there. How well I recollect one missionary couple passing some of their friends, saying: "We're going to the upper deck for a 'sundowner.' " This meant to pray before retiring.

God gave us such a beautiful sunset that evening of April 16, a peaceful afterglow in the heavens, tranquility, peace of God hovering near us, and we fell asleep in His arms for the night. The chapter of our life on the *Zamzam* had almost been written.

Next day was to write the fateful end of the *Zamzam* there in the South Atlantic, but in our hearts He engraved the "mercies of God" in His miraculous deliverance. And so on April 17 our "home" for one month was to pass into traceless oblivion, and we were made to realize that here we have no abiding place, and only the *things of God shall abide forever.*

THE RAINBOW DAWN

When thou passeth through the waters,
I will be with thee. Isaiah 43. 2.

I heard one of our missionaries speak about seven miracles in connection with their *Zamzam* journey. These were some of them:

That although fifty-five shots were fired at the *Zamzam* by the German raider, only nine reached the mark; yet the Germans are said to be good marksmen.

That although nine shells struck the *Zamzam*, no one aboard was killed. A few were injured. Most of the passengers were missionaries, but none of the missionaries was wounded, except that Mrs. Danielson received a cut from stepping on broken glass.

That although so many were cast into the open sea, among them several small children, no one was drowned. Every life was saved.

Each survivor had his or her own experiences that strange morning. No one can tell what his neighbor, in the presence of apparent death, thought and felt. We have therefore asked each one of our missionaries to tell us in his own way what he saw and lived through during those fateful moments.

MEETING A WARSHIP IN THE SOUTH ATLANTIC

DR. C. EINAR NORBERG

There had been some speculation among the passengers over the possibility of running into a German surface raider or submarine. We had legitimate reasons to be concerned about just such an eventuality, especially because the *Zam-*

zam was traveling without lights at night. Its strange behavior in suddenly turning about and altering its course on April 14, after picking up a mysterious wireless message, gave real substance to some of the speculations. The passengers were kept in complete ignorance about world events, which gave added prestige to rumors. We saw the two press representatives, who had joined us at Pernambuco, calling on the captain in the latter's cabin quite often. No news of any unusual character came down to the rest of us even through these men. It did, however, charge the air with a mysterious sense of a possible impending danger. It was therefore not a complete surprise to some of us when early on April 17, the sound of shrieking shells split the air over us. If anyone slept through the sound of the first shell, they did not sleep after the second salvo came over, which followed the first within fifteen to twenty seconds.

There were no alarm signals or any orders to take to the lifeboats. The shelling became intense and lasted probably ten minutes in all.

After first disposing of the admiralty code book, messages, and other important papers from his safe, Captain Smith finally signalled the identity of his ship. The warship ceased firing immediately upon receiving this flashlight signal. In the meanwhile many passengers had been wounded, a few quite severely.

A number of people began to abandon the ship during the shelling. Each one had to decide for himself what to do. It was very difficult to know, while the shelling continued, which would be the wisest procedure, to stay in the cabin or to get out and away from the ship as soon as possible. No one could predict just where the next shell would hit, so one place had to be considered as unsafe as the other. Some took time to dress fully while others left in their night clothes.

The noise was terrifying and the uncertainty of how long the *Zamzam* would keep afloat under such punishment drove the majority of the people to seek refuge in the lifeboats. A few children were separated from their parents in the process of taking to the lifeboats. One child was left dangling on a rope ladder near the water when the lifeboat into which she had intended to land was pushed out from the ship and rowed away. The little girl had to climb up to the deck and seek out another lifeboat. Many of the lifeboats had been damaged and did not keep out water. Several had to be abandoned. Heads were seen bobbing up and down in the sea all about the listing *Zamzam*.

One boat capsized, throwing all its occupants into the sea. In this boat had been Mrs. Danielson and her six children and Rev. Hult, who were left in the water until the German warship came and picked them up. It was not a very hopeful picture to behold. The thought of sharks came to our minds with all the possible horrible consequences. The uncertainty of any help coming from a warship which had just treated us so brutally with high-explosive shells, did not brighten our prospects.

Our long-planned-for trip to Africa had suddenly come to an end. The equipment and all our supplies were on the slowly sinking *Zamzam*. We thought of the many prayers friends and we had sent up to God about our safety on our way to the needy fields in Africa. Yes, we were in the valley, when with the rising sun we saw God's sign of promise in the sky: a clear and beautiful *rainbow*. What a lesson that silent arch in the sky taught us that morning. "Though I walk in the valley of the shadow of death, I shall fear no evil, for thou art with me."

THE "ZAMZAM" IS ATTACKED

MRS. V. EUGENE JOHNSON

"Grant to little children
Visions bright of Thee;
Guard the sailors tossing
O'er the deep blue sea."

This evening prayer seemed still to echo in my heart the fateful morning of April 17, at 5:30 o'clock. Only a few of the two hundred passengers and the one hundred and thirty members of the crew were awake when the shells from the surface raider began to hit the ship. While most of the thirty-five children aboard continued in carefree slumber, the adults awakened to the grim reality that death was coming close to them. Many of the passengers were too stunned to realize that swift action was necessary. Others who had encountered similar dangers before realized that the time for both prayer and action had come.

One mother spoke quietly to her ten-year-old son as she helped him into his lifeboat: "The Lord may spare us for further service, but if He wants to take us to His home now, we are ready, are we not, son?"

With a smile of confidence he replied, "Yes, Mother, we can trust Jesus always."

Our cabin was on the port side which faced the raider. When I jumped up on my older son's berth in order to close the porthole, I caught a glimpse of the raider and saw a flash as another shell was aimed at us. However, this shell fell short of its target and landed in the deep sea. Before I could arouse our four-year-old from his peaceful slumber, a shell struck less than twenty feet from us. This tore a huge hole in the side of the ship five feet below the waterline and caused the *Zamzam* to list heavily toward the port side. The smell of sulphur and the continued firing alarmed us. No word of direction came to us. Our cabin was next to the rear deck. When I opened the door I heard yelling and screaming on the upper deck aft. Some of the Egyptian crew were clamoring around lifeboat No. 10 to which we had been assigned. The deck was deserted. In my haste I concluded that the other passengers had awakened earlier and that only a few persons were left on the sinking *Zamzam*.

I told my husband that I could manage our two sons, Victor, age ten, and David, age four, so that he might render assistance to others who might be left on the ship. The noise of the shelling prevented him from hearing me. Victor was calm and brave. David was not fully awake, so I carried him up the steep iron ladder reserved for emergencies. As we crossed an open gangway leading to the rear of the ship, I helped David up and waved so the attackers might see there were children aboard. "Dear Lord, help our enemies to have compassion on us!" I prayed. The next shell passed over the ship. We climbed into the lifeboat assigned to us and crouched low as the firing continued.

We saw the terrible damage done by several shells which hit the ship, and we marvelled that our *Zamzam* did not become a blazing inferno. A Catholic priest entered the lifeboat. He was busy with his rosary, while the Mohammedan crew called loudly on Allah to save them. It seemed that hours had passed since the shelling began, and we had run for the lifeboat. The shelling ceased, and still my husband did not appear. In halting French I asked the priest if he had seen the father of Victor and David.

"Yes. I'm a holy father," he replied.

The shouting Egyptians prevented further conversation. They tried to pull the lifeboat away, but we heard other passengers calling and we forced the crew to hold the ropes while mothers, fathers, and their children, climbed down the ladder and sought for a place in the crowded lifeboat.

The *Zamzam*. Built in 1910. 8,299 tons. Photo copied from a British magazine by V. Eugene Johnson.

Finally, my husband also arrived and told us of his search for us and the fate of other passengers on the starboard side. We had left two older children in U.S.A. After commending them to the Lord, I told our ever-present Saviour, "Lord, if our task on earth is finished, prepare us and the children whom Thou hast given us for Thy home above."

The Lord never fails those who trust Him. A beautiful rainbow to remind us of His great promises arched the southern sky.

Our thoughts were with dear friends and fellow passengers, who were floating around in their lifebelts. Some clung to pieces of wreckage, others joined hands and encouraged one another. God gave us the assurance that He was ruling the winds and waves, and that we were kept in the hollow of His hand. Lifeboat No. 10 pulled slowly out to sea. When we reached over to examine the food box, we discovered that there was no food and no fresh water to drink.

Some time later we discovered that our adversaries intended to rescue us from the watery deep. None of us knew his fate. The *Tamesis*, the raider which had fired fifty-five shells at the *Zamzam*, drew near and we heard orders to come alongside. Then I had to ask God to forgive me for once saying that I had rather be dead than to be a prisoner of war.

It was a great relief to learn that the wounded were being treated, and that already more than one hundred persons had been rescued from the water. Though our dry lips uttered no sound, our hearts sang songs of deliverance. When a basket was lowered and he was requested to climb in, little David made his first protest. He did not want to leave Mummy, Dad, and Brother, and ride in a dark basket to an unknown destiny. He was less reluctant to try the new venture when he learned that some of his playmates had preceded him. He even said, "Thank you," when assisted into the basket.

I had taken a small case of necessities and a blanket with me, but I could not retain my hold on them as I climbed the swaying ladder. When I smiled and said, "Bitte," to the guard he lowered a rope and my bundle was brought up. The inspectors returned it to me without opening it.

"Where are my children?" was the first question I asked of the guard after I had thanked him for untying the rope which had enabled me to climb.

"I'm here, Mother," called Victor from a near-by hatch. "David has been taken downstairs. The guard told me to wait here. I'll be O.K., if you want to go to little brother."

I gave my brave little helper a hug and told him to be patient while I searched for the little one. I was directed below, but my knees began to shake as I walked down one flight of iron steps after the other. It became hotter and hotter as I descended to a room filled with women and children. There I found my baby David.

In searching for Mrs. Danielson and her six children, who had been floating around in the water, I first found our two Augustana teachers, who were busy encouraging weary mothers and frightened, silent children. I had opportunity to notice the scores of wooden bunks which filled about three-fourths of the room space. Each bunk was furnished with a mattress and a pillow of straw. Some names were written with white chalk on a number of bunks. When I saw "Kinnan and Peter" written on one, and "Olson and Wendy" on another bunk, I realized that the two Levitt children, whose mother had been severely wounded, would be well cared for.

The Danielson children were in need of clothes and food after their exposure in the water, and they smiled as our little emergency case yielded sweaters, gum, and a few sticks of candy. The other members of our party joined us in thanking the Lord that He had heard our call for help and saved us from a worse fate.

"O give thanks unto the Lord, for he is good."

OVERTAKEN BY A GERMAN RAIDER

MRS. C. EINAR NORBERG

I had awakened early, and I was lying on my bunk meditating, when I heard a peculiar whine over the ship. Immediately my husband jumped up, saying, "Get up! We are being shelled!" He helped the two children, who were sleeping on the upper bunks to get down. Then he told us in a calm voice to take time to dress warmly and not to leave the cabin, as no signal had been given to do so.

The shells were coming over in quick succession now. Whenever one would hit our ship she would shudder and shake. The air was filled with the deafening sound of the bursting shells. I looked out of the porthole but once. There was the raider headed right for us. As I looked it seemed two guns fired. Those shells hit short of us, striking the water quite near.

God gave us the strength needed for that hour. As we were dressing, our son said: "Daddy, let's pray!" It was harder for our seven-year-old daughter to remain calm. I had just gotten a New Testament and the small portraits of my parents buttoned into a vest pocket, when a shell struck. It ripped through a couple of cabins and a corridor not many feet away. Our Ruth screamed, "Daddy, they'll shoot us!" After this explosion our corridor filled with smoke. We decided we must leave for our lifeboat.

Upon reaching the lifeboat station, we found that the boat had already been lowered into the water. It was well filled with members of the Egyptian crew, though very few of the passengers assigned to this boat were there. We proceeded to climb down the swaying rope ladder into the boat.

The *Zamzam* was listing to portside. We never knew at what moment she might roll over. Later the pumps were started. This helped straighten up the old ship for a few more hours of passive duty, before she was violently "spurlos versenkt."

We were a rather apprehensive group sitting in lifeboat No. 10. The men had to supervise the Egyptian crew in maneuvering the boat. Looming before us was the *Tamesis*, the ship which had deliberately caused our plight. We felt so small. All about us we saw people floating in the sea, the kapok lifebelts saving the many who did not know how to swim. Several boats had filled with water or capsized, thus forcing the people into the open sea. We did not know to what extent this calamity had brought death and suffering to our friends. Suddenly someone called our attention to God's promise shining in the sky! That beautiful *rainbow* seemed to speak words of comfort and trust as it appeared to embrace us in its calm majesty. God, not only a German raider, was near!

Soon we saw an officer on the *Tamesis* beckoning to us. We drew up close enough to hear him give the orders in English: "Come up alongside, please. We are taking you aboard." So we were not to remain in this little lifeboat without food and water. But what was to be our destiny after we had once been taken on board this German ship?

"*In God have I put my trust, I will not be afraid;*
What can man do unto me?"

Psalm 56. 11.

SHELLING OF THE "ZAMZAM"

REV. V. EUGENE JOHNSON

God is our refuge and strength,
A very present help in trouble.

It was on Thursday, April 17, at 5:30 in the morning, that the attack on the *Zamzam* occurred. Most of the passengers were still asleep in their cabins. A few were already up and dressed. The only warning given was the explosion of the first shell fired from a distance of about three and a half miles. It was quite sufficient to awaken me and to make me aware of what was happening. It brought back vivid recollections of the last World War, in which I served for almost two years.

Other shells followed in quick succession, exploding with terrific force, some falling short of the ship, others passing harmlessly overhead, and nine of them hitting the ship, until, as we later learned from the chief gunner of the attacking ship, fifty-five shots had been fired.

As I awoke I cried to my wife and two sons, Victor, age ten, and David, age four: "Get up, quick! We're being shelled. Dress and put on your lifebelts." Even as I spoke shells exploded near by with such terrific detonations that we could hardly hear each other speak. Even so, my wife and son Victor acted with amazing coolness and self-control. David was too young to realize what was happening. In a few moments all of us were dressed and trussed up in our life preservers.

At first we thought our safest refuge was right in our cabin. But our cabin was located on the side of the ship nearest to the attacking raider, and when a shell struck near our cabin five feet below the waterline, causing the *Zamzam* to list heavily to port, we feared that the ship might suddenly roll over on its side, entrapping us like rats in our cabin. We decided to proceed to the lifeboat to which we had been assigned, No. 10 on the rear port deck. As we crossed an open hatch, I saw the raider in the distance, a grey silhouette against the morning horizon.

I determined to return to our cabin to secure our passport and moneybelt, and told my wife and children to go on to the lifeboat where I would rejoin them in a few moments. Hurriedly dragging out our steamer trunk from beneath one of the lower berths, I had it open in a flash and was digging among the contents for our passport and moneybelt when a shell struck with a deafening explosion about eighteen feet away, and immediately I heard cries of pain and calls for help.

Having obtained the objects of my search I rushed out into the corridor and discovered three men lying in pools of blood only a few feet away. They were Francis Vicovari, of the British-American Ambulance Corps, who had suffered a compound fracture of the right femur, a dislocated knee, and a deep flesh wound in the left leg, a shattered right ankle, and a broken upper right arm, as well as severe lacerations in other parts of his body; Dr. Robt. Starling, chiropractor, who had received a broken femur, deep flesh wounds in the left leg, deep lacerations and a broken ankle in the right leg; and Muhamed Baburi, an Egyptian member of the crew, who had suffered a deep wound in his abdomen and head injuries. Several other passengers reached the wounded men at the same time that I did and requested me to summon a physician, of which there were nine among the passengers.

This I did and afterward went to find my family, but could not discover them in the lifeboat to which we had been assigned. It had already been lowered, but passengers were still descending into it by means of a rope ladder. The

Egyptian crew members in charge of it shouted vociferously at each other and because of this I suppose my calls to my wife and children could not be heard. So I went in search of them, calling at all the various lifeboat stations on both the lower and upper decks, but to no avail.

By this time the firing had ceased and I had opportunity to see close at hand some of the destruction wrought by the shells, which were of six- or eight-inch caliber. The port side of the lounge was blown to shreds, likewise other parts of the bridge. One shot had torn a huge hole right through the funnel. Another had hit the radio cabin, making it impossible to broadcast an S.O.S. This was a blessing in disguise, as the captain of the raider later told us that if such a distress message had been sent out, he would have sunk the *Zamzam* at once, in which case we probably would have been left to our fate, either to perish by drowning or from thirst and exposure in open lifeboats. Another shell had completely destroyed one of the lifeboats. Another of the lifeboats could not even be launched. So the people assigned to these boats had to seek room elsewhere. When two of the lifeboats, filled with people, were lowered into the water, they swamped, having been punctured by shrapnel, so that the occupants had to depend on their life preservers for support. Yet another lifeboat was dropped several feet with such force that when it struck the water it capsized, with the result that from these three lifeboats there were between 150 and 180 people floating around in the ocean, being kept afloat by their lifebelts. Among them were Pastor Ralph Hult and Mrs. Lillian Danielson with her six children, the youngest less than two years old and too small to wear a lifebelt. Lois Danielson had to be tied about the neck of her brave mother, who managed to keep her children together like little ducklings in a big pond. I finally returned to the lifeboat to which we had been assigned, but not until

I had taken several pictures of the approaching raider, and of the people getting into the lifeboats.

When I came to our own lifeboat I was overjoyed to discover our son Victor in it. In answer to my shouted inquiry he pointed out my wife and son David huddled in the bottom. In a moment I was over the rail of the *Zamzam* and down the rope ladder to rejoin them. Just in time, too, before the Egyptians pulled away. In some instances the Egyptians rowed the lifeboats away, leaving passengers dangling at the very end of the rope ladders.

I shall never forget the sight of all those people, men, women and children, floating around in the water. At the time we did not know if the raider would come to our assistance. My faith tells me that there was Somebody walking on the surface of the deep among those bobbing heads, even as He did centuries ago on the Sea of Galilee, hearing also the cries of those men, women and children, even as He heard the cry of Peter: "Lord, save me, I perish." It was because of Him that there was no loss of life.

It was not long before the raider had approached close enough so that we could hear an officer at the rail ordering the lifeboats to pull up alongside where the occupants would be taken aboard. The raider, whose name we now discovered to be the *Tamesis*, also launched several motorboats which cruised about picking up the people in the water. Lastly they removed the passengers and members of the crew that were still aboard the *Zamzam*, and by seven o'clock everybody was safe on the *Tamesis*.

It was a miracle of God that though fifty-five shells had been fired, of which nine struck the *Zamzam*, only nine persons were wounded, and only three of them very seriously, and among the nine not one Protestant missionary or member of his family. According to latest information the three wounded most seriously are recovering.

WHEN DEATH WAS IMMINENT

ESTHER M. OLSON

On the Thursday morning after Easter, we were awakened at dawn by a sound as of a dynamite explosion. We slipped on coats, shoes, lifebelts and hurried into the passageway. It was filled with people, white of face, but not in panic.

Another blast! And then another, so violent that we were left limp and shaking.

A man stood at the deck door in the upper passageway and warned us to remain inside until the shelling ceased. We kneeled there in that dimly lit hall, waiting, praying.

Many ask, "What did you think that morning?" Well I remember! Was there any sin in my heart that had not been confessed to God and washed away in the precious blood of Jesus? I prayed, "Dear Lord Jesus, forgive me, cleanse me, take me home now for Thy dear name's sake."

It is wonderful to know each day that Jesus is my own personal Saviour, but when death was imminent then nothing else made any difference. It was *Jesus only*.

Suddenly the shooting was over, and the guard said, "Go to your lifeboats." When we reached ours, it had been lowered into the water. The poor Egyptian crew was frenzied with fear. They cut the ropes and rowed away before our boat was nearly filled. Families were separated, and it was heartrending to hear parents beg them to return to the *Zamzam* for their children. Mrs. Muir prayed aloud. Trustfully she claimed the promises, "I will never leave thee nor forsake thee, I will hold thee in the hollow of my hand."

Suddenly I looked up and saw the huge sinister raider that had shelled us. An officer called down to us, inviting us to come aboard. We obeyed.

PASSING THROUGH THE WATERS

REV. RALPH D. HULT

But now thus saith the Lord . . . : Fear not, for I have redeemed thee; I have called thee by thy name, thou art mine. When thou passeth through the waters, I will be with thee. . . . Fear not; for I am with thee. . . . Thus saith the Lord, who maketh a way in the sea, and a path in the mighty waters. Isaiah 43.

In the early morning of April 17 I was suddenly awakened by a "*bang.*"

It seemed as though a huge wave slapped the ship and dashed over the deck.

What could it be? I could not look out as the glass in the porthole of our cabin had been painted. The sea seemed to be calm. No, it could not be a wave.

With such thoughts flashing through my mind, I arose.

"*Wham—Bang!*"

Overhead and toward the front of the ship I heard things crashing and falling. Now it dawned on me what all the confusion was about. Our ship was being shelled.

One of my two cabin mates had arisen very early that morning. He came rushing in, and we asked him what was happening.

His answer was, "A raider!"

A moment later we heard another "*Wham—Bang.*"

Now the light in our cabin became quite dim, and for a few moments it seemed as though we were doomed to go down in darkness. There was no time to lose.

The other cabin mate and I dressed hurriedly. As we stepped out of the cabin we saw two of our neighbors lying helpless at the foot of the near-by stairway. We paused to see if we could help and found that the two wounded men were being cared for by their companions. The long, narrow corridor was full of frightened passengers trying to get out, but there was no panic. As we were slowly working our way out of the place, we were relieved to observe that the shelling had ceased.

When we finally reached the open space on our deck, near the rear hatch, we could distinguish the dark form of a ship in the distance. Signal lights were flashing from it.

Our lifeboat station was on the deck above, so we had to climb a narrow and steep outside stairway. Many were trying to get up this stairway, so we made very slow progress, but at last we reached the upper deck. As we approached our station we saw the Egyptians lowering the boat from the boatdeck above. When it reached the level of our deck the women and children were helped into it, among them Mrs. Danielson and her children. Two of the boats on our side of the ship had been destroyed by the shelling, so there was considerable crowding at our station. When the boat had been filled to its capacity the sailors shouted, "No more, no more!" And we were lowered to the water.

As soon as the ropes that held our boat were unloosed we noticed that it was taking water. The seamen were asked to refasten the ropes, but they insisted that we would be able to bail out the water.

The oars were worked and we moved toward the stern of the sinking *Zamzam*.

In a few minutes we were up to our knees in water, and it was evident that our boat had been very badly damaged. It was impossible to bail out the water fast enough. In the excitement there was some shifting of positions in the boat, and suddenly it turned over! How thankful we were to the Ruler of wind and wave that the sea was calm!

As the boat turned over some of its occupants were thrown some distance. As I was one of the last to enter the boat I was near the rudder and so just slipped into the water. At no time did I go under.

I do not swim, and so I was very grateful for the support of my life preserver and an oar which floated within my reach. I soon managed to get near enough to the overturned boat to grasp one of the rope loops on its side.

As soon as I felt myself anchored in this way to the boat I thought of Mrs. Danielson and her children. What a relief it was to see them near by, all still afloat! But how long could they stay above water?

As I saw that brave mother with her youngest gripped in the crook of her left arm, my soul cried out to Almighty God for help. And I also pleaded with the Egyptian seamen, who had managed to crawl up on the overturned boat, and now sat there with uplifted arms calling on Allah, to lower their hands and try to reach the children and draw them out of the water. They did succeed in reaching some of the children, thank God!

"What next?" was the question in our minds, as we managed to close in around our overturned lifeboat. How long could we hold out, floating about in the ocean?

As we looked in the direction of the raider, we observed that it was slowly moving toward us. It also seemed as though we were drifting toward the approaching warship. After a while we found ourselves right at its side, and were in danger of being caught in its propellers.

Thank God, the German sailors were trying to reach us with ropes. After several efforts we managed to hold fast to their ropes and as soon as the raider's lifeboats could be lowered they came to our rescue. How wonderful it seemed to feel strong arms draw us out of the water!

Thank God, our feet had found a footing again!

The small children were lifted up to the ship's deck in a rope basket. The older children and the grownups climbed up on a rope ladder. The occupants of our boat were the first to reach the raider's deck.

As we stood there watching our fellow passengers and the crew members one after the other arriving on the deck, our hearts sang praises to God for His deliverance. Surely, He had been very near, "a very present help," as we passed through the waters that morning. Had He not intervened in our behalf? The very hands that but a little while ago were wielding those terrible instruments of destruction were now efficiently ministering to our needs.

"With courage, strength and hope renewed" we beheld His glorious sun rising in the direction of the great Dark Continent. In the western sky we beheld a glorious bow, arching the sky.

THE SINKING OF THE "ZAMZAM"

VELURA KINNAN

You have heard of the sad fate of the *Zamzam*, the holy ship, "the ship that could never sink," but I will tell you my own story of the disaster.

It was just at dawn on the morning of April 17 that we were shocked from our sleep by a violent blow that struck broadside on the *Zamzam*. It fell like a bolt from a giant hand. The boat shook from one end to the other. I knew at once what it meant. The enemy had attacked! The end had come! We sprang from our beds and began to work as if our actions had been preplanned. The shells pounded at short, irregular intervals. No one spoke. We prayed silently.

It is at times like this that one learns what is really important. Now I knew it was not necessary to try to save anything. Now only the riches one had in heaven made any difference. It was not necessary to try to dress. Now only the Lord's robe of righteousness was really important.

We just stepped into the shoes beside the bed, slipped on warm coats and tied on our lifebelts as we hurried from the cabin. Another shell! We started for the lifeboats, not that we expected to be saved, but only that we might be obedient and faithful to the end. People in various stages of dress rushed through the corridor. All were mute and silent. Another blow! Esther fell! She was white, but not hurt! We helped her up and rushed to the corridor leading to the lifeboat. It was filled with people, tense and still.

Someone at the door took command shouting, "Do not leave the corridor until the shelling stops! Get down on the floor and fortify yourselves for the next blow!" We did. It came soon. It was hard to tell which was the harder to bear, the tense minutes between the blows or the falling of the shells themselves.

There was no hysteria. A churchly hush filled the room. We were waiting for death. People prayed softly. We searched our hearts for unconfessed sin and gave thanks for the blood of Jesus that can cleanse from all unrighteousness, for we most truly believed we were soon to close our eyes upon this world and to open them in His eternal kingdom.

At last, there came a long silence. We waited. Could it be that after all the effort they had made to sink our boat and take our lives, that now they had ceased to fire and there was yet a chance for our safety. It seemed impossible! The silence continued. Now the same voice commanded again, "Everyone to your lifeboats!" We moved quickly to our places.

Now came hysteria. The entire crew of the *Zamzam* were Egyptians. Mohammedans they were. They, too, believed that death was real, and death was near, and they did not have that hope which is "built on nothing less than Jesus' blood and righteousness." And what a difference that makes! They worked excitedly with the ropes, shouting wildly as they worked, and somehow it seemed the ropes would not do what they had planned. And well they might be excited, for one lifeboat was entirely destroyed and two others were filled with holes. At last the boat was down, and we began to fill it. When only half the passengers had taken their places, the excited crew cut loose and began to row away from the badly crippled boat. No sooner had we started than a distressed father and mother began to plead with the crew to return for their child who had been left on the slowly sinking boat, but in vain. The Egyptians could not understand the pleading, and were too excited to return if they had. I shall never forget the look of anguish on the faces of the father and mother as they prayed, commending their little one to God's care and keeping, as we rowed farther and farther away from the boat.

Just then I looked behind to see one of the lifeboats pour its human cargo out into the shark-infested sea. The sight of those heads bobbing up and down in the water so sickened me that I could not look again. I turned my back upon the scene and looked out upon a beautiful morning. The sea was calm and smooth and beautiful and blue. The sun was just beginning to rise and the heavens overhead were spanned by a beautiful rainbow. Truly the Man of Galilee was present there that day, proving Himself according to His promise, "A refuge and a strength and a very present help in time of trouble."

I looked up now and for the first time I could see our enemy, a German surface raider, a sinister gray monster. The decks were lined with sailors. The Nazi flag fluttered defiantly in the breeze. As I watched them moving swiftly down upon us, I wondered, "Have they come nearer that they may complete their destruction, or will they rescue us?"

We soon found out, for a man with a megaphone stepped to the rail and called, "Draw alongside and come on board."

We had heard what was the fate of those who fell into enemy hands, but there was no alternative. We must go on board! We soon found ourselves climbing up the side of the vessel that only a few short minutes before had been pouring death and destruction upon us. What would our fate be once we had reached the top?

THE RAINBOW DAWN

MRS. ELMER R. DANIELSON

I had just awakened, and lay in bed musing: "This is the seventeenth of April, only four more days to Capetown, and letters from our daddy!"

Oh, what a crash! Was it thunder, or what?

I rushed to the open door of the deck, and looked out to see if a storm were approaching, and surely enough the very stormclouds of Hitler loomed ominously near only a few miles distant in the form of a raider. Another terrific bang! I saw the fire spurt, and felt the reverberations above us.

My little ones, sleeping in the next cabin, came running in with: "Mommy, what is it? What shall we do?"

I answered, "An enemy boat is firing at us. You little children try to be brave in Jesus. Help get your lifebelts on tight. Hurry!"

There were more terrific explosions, above us, below us, to the sides of us, the whole ship shuddered from the onslaught. Another bang right above our room. Clatter! Clatter! Water pitchers, tumblers, mirrors above the lavatories cracked and fell to the floor. The lights waned, the

Survivor-ladened lifeboat pulls away from the doomed ship. Photo by *Life* magazine.

blackouts were still on, the ship listed, the bullets whizzed. We heard moaning of wounded passengers in the distance. It was gruesome, the terrific noise from without, the frightened smallest trio crying within, objecting strenuously to those bumpy life jackets tied around their chests.

If I ever wished our daddy were there to help during our trip it was *this* morn, but he was thousands of miles away. Our heavenly Father was present though in a very real way, and when I almost despaired: "It's no use! We're lost!" God just steeled me anew, turned my face up into His, gave me the needed strength and led us each step of the way.

Just then the assistant purser came running into our room, blood on his cheek near his eye.

"Can you get out of here?" he asked.

"Yes. We're almost ready, but I've heard no signal. We'll manage all right."

Then commending ourselves to God, and praying an immeasurable faith for our daddy whatever happened to us that morning, we hurried to our lifeboat station.

Reaching our lifeboat I remembered the necessary sun-helmets and my purse with the passport, and I darted back to get them, but I had only gone a few yards when six frantic little voices pleaded: "Mommy, don't go back! You'll be left! Come!"

That was too much, and I rejoined them. Maybe we would need no passport except to the heavenly shore and Jesus had already granted it. We crawled over the railing into the lifeboat, and slowly it was lowered by unwinding a pole. When almost down to the water, the rope slipped and hit me on the head. How our Father protected me that I was not stunned and rendered helpless for the next half-hour's adventure, even if two bumps soon raised on my head! A couple of belated passengers came down the rope ladder, and we pushed out from the *Zamzam*. But, oh! our lifeboat had no doubt been hit by shrapnel. It was like a sieve. We tried to attract the attention of folks still on the *Zamzam*, but they were rushing to the lifeboat stations on the opposite side. No one saw our plight.

We drifted just past the stern of the boat a short distance when one man called out, "We're sunk, that's all."

With one more look full into the face of Jesus, with a "Thy will be done," I clasped Lois Christine, our baby, more firmly in my left arm, grabbed Wilfred's hand with my right, called to Laurence to try to watch Luella, and then with "Keep praying in your hearts, my little ones, Jesus loves you all. We're safe in Him whatever happens," we all went into the deep as the boat just went out from under us since it had filled completely. What a feeling! To go down into the shadow of the valley of death with these six treasures! But Jesus went with us all the way! In our spirits we were able to sing:

> "In the tempests of life, on its wide, heaving sea,
> Thou blest Rock of Ages, I'm hiding in Thee."

Believers and unbelievers, and "from the cradle to the grave" passengers floated along together. Even the lifeboat now bobbed up, bottom side up, and before long Luella and Wilfred were hoisted on top of it, guarded by Ali, an Egyptian. Everyone in our group of some thirty-five stayed in a nucleus by the lifeboat. Some held on to its edges, and bobbed up and down with it in the billows. Fellow passengers were kind to me. One man pushed an oar under my arm for me to rest upon occasionally as my love burden grew heavier.

The men motioned the raider for help, but one of our group said: "They won't help a feller after all this."

To my surprise I saw the raider make toward us, and a motor launch was lowered over its side. But alas! They made for the other capsized lifeboat.

What! no help for us yet? How much longer can we hold out?"

Now a second motor launch was lowered over the side of the raider and came in our direction. Soon it arrived. The little children were put in first, then women and men clambered into the launch. Chug, chug! We were on our way to the raider. We stopped just below the big rope ladder dangling over the side of the *Tamesis*.

Guards came down to help the children and women up. Once on the top deck, a German officer took off our soaked life belts, and turning to me said: "Follow me into a warm room."

I replied: "I can't until all my children are safe."

He looked at the four children near by who called me Mother and asked: "Mein Gott! One, two, three, four. Are there more?" It seemed his voice had a sense of guilt and sympathy for having helped to plunge us into this fate.

Now some familiar voices from below in the launch called out: "They're coming up, Mrs. Danielson," and just then a straw basket bag was hoisted over the railing and placed at my feet. I peeped inside and there with outstretched arms and "Mommy" on her lips, those big brown eyes of Lois Christine pleaded I take her.

Another basket came over the edge and in it sat Wilfred, drenched like a kitten, shivering and blue, but a big smile stole across his face as he saw that he was up high and safe, out of the big "pond." When my big son had come up, a young German marine, just twenty, had said: "We didn't want to do it, my boy, but it was *orders*." Already Sonny felt a touch of humanity in the youth, forced to serve against the dictates of his heart.

We were led to a warm cabin. The children's wet clothing was removed, and they huddled three or four into a bed under warm blankets, munching some chocolates and cookies the guards had given them. Having seen them safely to bed, my strength was spent. I just dropped on my knees there beside their bed, and thanked God for saving us, for truly without Him that morning we would have perished. A German guard soon gently touched me on the shoulder as I knelt there sobbing in prayer, and showed me a chair. He did not understand that I had now found real rest for my soul after that *awful* experience, the *glorious* experience of proving Jesus true to the end. I looked at my six priceless jewels and how rich I felt! The earthly values I had left on the *Zamzam* were *nothing* compared to the riches God saved for Daddy and myself in our little ones.

God drew us all nearer Himself that early April dawn, and the covenant of His love, a most gorgeous rainbow, stretched across the sky just beyond the *Tamesis.* How we thank and praise the Holy Triune for that "Rainbow Dawn." May it truly be said of us:

"*Saved to serve.*"

ON THE "TAMESIS"

V. EUGENE JOHNSON

If it had not been Jehovah who was on our side, . . .
Then they had swallowed us up alive, . . .
Then the waters had overwhelmed us. Psalm 124. 2–4.

Small children were hoisted aboard the German raider by means of baskets at the end of long ropes. Older children and adults had to climb aboard up rope ladders. A few women as well as most of the wounded persons had to be helped aboard, some of the latter in tight-laced stretchers.

The women and children were taken aboard first and with the exception of a few of the older children were sent below deck at once. The men were permitted to walk about in a small restricted portion of the ship, where we were soon called upon to line up to register our names and citizenship and the name of our nearest kin not on the ship, and to surrender our passports, money, flashlights, large knives, cameras, field glasses, compasses, matches, and revealing papers, if we had any.

About midafternoon the women and children began to appear on the deck and the men were ordered below for breakfast and lunch combined in one meal of a thick stew of rice and vegetables, tea without sugar or milk, and buttered coarse dark brown bread. The women and children had already partaken of a somewhat similar repast, except that they received white bread.

After finishing this meal we were all allowed up on deck again, where those who had been in the water had an opportunity to dry their wet clothes, mostly without removing them from their bodies. Meanwhile launches from the

German ship continued to make trip after trip to the *Zamzam*, first bringing loose clothing, afterward suitcases, trunks, typewriters, and other baggage which the sailors found in the staterooms and cabins of the passengers and officers. They brought aboard also a large amount of the ship's supplies, such as food, cigarettes, soap, and other goods. As we saw some of our belongings brought aboard we felt greatly cheered by the prospect of receiving them back again.

I offered my services to the German officers to go aboard the *Zamzam* to help fetch my own and others' belongings, but my offer was politely rejected with the statement that the German sailors would make a thorough search of every cabin, and bring aboard the *Tamesis* all that they found. Whether they actually did this we do not know, but many of the passengers received only a small portion of their belongings back again when later on the contents of the various cabins were ostensibly restored to their rightful owners. Some received *nothing.* When we inquired about personal effects that we had actually seen brought aboard the raider, we were told that the matter would be investigated. Possibly it was, but we never received our belongings notwithstanding. Apparently nothing was removed from the holds of the *Zamzam.*

About 2:30 P.M. we were informed that the transfer had been completed and that the *Zamzam* was about to be sunk. Mr. David E. Scherman, staff photographer of *Life* magazine, and I applied for and received permission from the captain to have our cameras again and photograph the obsequies. I took movies and between us we took many still snaps of the ship as it went down. Later the Germans confiscated these as well as many other photographs which we took.

A single launch containing several German sailors was seen to pull away from the doomed ship and retire to a safe distance.

A few minutes later a deep, heavy boom from within the *Zamzam* announced that the first time bomb had exploded. Every survivor's heart was tense with emotion as we stood at the rail of the *Tamesis* and watched the tragedy.

In a few moments a second explosion, much louder than the first, sent a large column of water into the air from the forward hatch, and the bow of the ship began to settle.

A third blast about three minutes later caused a smaller column of water to rise out of the rear hatch and made the ship list so sharply to port that we expected it to roll over. The bow started to disappear first.

A dull explosion amidship, possibly from the boilers which by this time were almost cooled off, hastened the sinking. The funnel broke off as it began to submerge.

Probably about ten minutes after the first internal explosion the *Zamzam* disappeared from view, churning the surface of the sea that claimed it, and leaving only scattered wreckage and debris to mark the spot where it had been a few minutes before.

Apart from the personal losses of the passengers and crew, the ship and its cargo were worth about $3,000,000. The personal losses of the passengers varied greatly. Four had new motorcars as well as much costly household equipment. One had a stamp collection valued at $2,500 in one of his trunks which went down. One of the officers of the *Tamesis*, interested in philately, actually shed tears when he heard this later. The equipment of The British-American Ambulance Corps included twenty ambulances and four other cars besides much other goods totaling in value over $75,000. The holds also contained thousands of dollars worth of equipment belonging to the various mission societies represented among the passengers. Though we could not but deeply regret these great losses, we were thankful beyond words that the sea would never be required to give up its dead on the *Zamzam.* Even "Willie," a dachshund belonging to one of the passengers, and the chief engineer's cat had been saved. So far as is known, two of the ship's cats and three parrots belonging to the crew accounted for the only loss of life. Yet it was a funeral that will always remain one of our most vivid memories.

Shortly after the sinking of the *Zamzam* we were all ordered below deck again, two floors down, where we were served our second meal of the day similar to the first and were assigned bunks for the night, women and children on one side and men on the other side of a large room which evidently served as quarters for additional crew members when necessary. Each bunk was furnished with an excelsior-filled mattress and pillow. Since the weather was warm, we felt no discomfort because we had no blankets or sheets. In fact, the temperature was too hot for us to desire either.

About midnight we were awakened by the sounding of the ship's siren, and many of the *Zamzam* passengers, particularly the mothers and children, became anxious lest they should have to go through another experience of being shot at and having to take to lifeboats. All exits from our quarters were securely locked. Through a small peep hole in an iron door we could see German sailors rushing up the stairway, carrying their lifebelts and gasmasks. But inquiries addressed to them brought no satisfaction. A German officer soon opened the door, however, and assured us that there was no cause for alarm. A ship had been sighted which they thought was one of their own to which we were to be transferred, and the warning had been sounded only as a matter of precaution. In case of real emergency we would not be left to perish like rats in a cage. Gradually the excitement died down, and everybody went to sleep again.

The next morning, after finishing our ablutions with salt water without benefit of soap or towel, in a crowded toilet room, and eating a breakfast of gruel, buttered bread, and tea without milk or sugar, we were again allowed up on deck and discovered at once that the German officer's explanation of the previous night's alarm was correct. Another ship about equal in size to the *Tamesis* was made fast to its stern by a heavy rope from the other ship's prow. Already launches were busy transporting baggage and supplies from the *Tamesis* to the new ship. This work continued until late afternoon. For lunch we were given a thin soup of rice, vegetables, and bits of corned beef, and the usual bread and tea. At the request of the captain of the *Tamesis*, whom we had not seen as yet, five persons were appointed to represent the main groups from the *Zamzam*, i.e., (1) one hundred and eight missionaries and members of their families; (2) seventeen Roman Catholic missionaries; (3) twenty-four members of The British-American Ambulance Corps; (4) the fifty-five remaining passengers; (5) the officers and crew of the *Zamzam*. This committee was duly invited into the office of the captain, who proved to be a large athletic man of about forty-five years and of very pleasant personality. Though at the time he carefully refrained from divulging his name, we later learned it to be Rogge. He was said to be a Lutheran. Speaking through an interpreter, he welcomed us most courteously and put us at our ease at once. He apologized for having shelled the *Zamzam*, and putting the passengers and crew into so much danger and discomfort. He justified his action, however, by the fact that the *Zamzam* was traveling completely blacked out, not even showing navigation lights, and by the fact that its outlines were identical with those of certain troop transports used by the British. We ourselves had already learned that the *Zamzam* had originally been *H.M.S. Leistershire*, built in 1910, and had served as a troop transport during the last World War. Therefore Captain Rogge had concluded that the *Zamzam* was a troop transport, possibly heavily armed. But when he had observed the signal transmitted in Morse code by Captain Wm. G. Smith by means of a flashlight from the bridge of the *Zamzam*, he had ordered his men to cease firing at once. He expressed deep personal regret over the entire tragedy. Personally I believe that he spoke sincerely. Nor could I deny the validity of much that he said in justification of his actions in attacking the *Zamzam*. I believe that the initial and a large share of the blame for the entire tragedy rests on the officers of the *Zamzam* and on the British Admirality under whose orders the ship was sailing.

Captain Rogge stated that he considered us his "guests" and not as prisoners of war, and that as far as circumstances would allow he would do his best to see to it that we were provided with all necessary comforts. We were about to be transferred to an unarmed German ship which would either transfer us to a ship of some neutral country or put us ashore in some neutral port as soon as possible. At the same time we were asked to remember that Germany was at war, and therefore the passengers would have to be governed by measures which were designed to insure the safety of the ship. Captain Rogge dismissed us with cordial handshaking and expressed the wish that he might some day have the pleasure of meeting us under more agreeable circumstances. The extent to which his promises were fulfilled will be seen in the continuation of our story.

A short time later we were introduced to the captain of the ship to which we were to be transferred, a man about the same age as Captain Rogge, but shorter and of a brusque, hard-boiled demeanor, who triumphantly greeted Captain Smith of the *Zamzam*, speaking in fairly good English:

"Vell, Captain, I'm de captain of dis odder ship," jerking his thumb toward the new ship. "If you fellows do as you're told, den everyting vill be all right. And if you don't, ve'll take care of dat, too." And with these words he stamped off.

In midafternoon all persons taken from the *Zamzam*, with the exception of the three men wounded most seriously, i.e., Mr. Frances Vicovari, Dr. Robt. Starling, and Mr. Ned Laughinghouse, whose condition was too serious for them to be moved, were transferred in launches to the new ship, whose name we then discovered to be the *Dresden*.

LIFE OF THE MEN ABOARD THE PRISON SHIP

REV. RALPH D. HULT

Thou didst cast me into the depth, in
the heart of the seas,
And the flood was round about me.
Jonah 2. 3.

St. Helena, the enforced home of Napoleon Bonaparte during the last years of his life, lies 1,200 miles west of the African coast. At a point about 750 miles south and a little west of that island the good ship *Zamzam* was sent to the bottom of the sea. From the deck of the man-of-war that had battered it so badly, we saw it sink into its watery grave in the early afternoon of April 17. We were stunned by the sad spectacle. Could it be true? Yes, it must be so. We saw the men, who had given the old ship the *coup de grace*, return, and then we were carried away from the place. We were carried into captivity. Whither, we knew not.

About twenty-four hours after the sinking of the *Zamzam* we were transferred to another vessel. It bore the name *Dresden*, but to us, who thus became its enforced passengers, it has become known as "the prison ship." We have been informed that in peaceful times it plied between Europe and South America. It seems quite probable that the outbreak of the present war found it in some South American port. In the hope of eventually reaching its home port it had again put to sea and was at present serving as supply ship to the raider *Tamesis*. It was a freighter type vessel, but had accommodations for about thirty-five passengers. One could not but sympathize with the captain of the *Dresden* when in the afternoon of April 18 about ten times that number were placed aboard his ship. Of those, eighty-seven were women and children. There we were, in the South Atlantic, about midway between South America and Africa. In whatever direction we might go we would be in danger of capture, or even destruction, by enemies of the Nazi and Fascist regime. Captain Jaeger had to cope with some very vital problems, but he and his officers did their part well.

As we came up the gangway of the *Dresden* the women and children were sent to the upper deck amidships, and the men were ordered below the hatches in the fore part of the ship. As ninety-one male passengers and nineteen officers of the *Zamzam* slowly descended the newly constructed stairway, leading from hatch No. 2 into the hold below, they were a bewildered and forlorn lot. There they found themselves in a bare room, 54x54 feet. The steel floor was covered with loose planks. The wall toward the bow of the ship was of steel plate and the wall toward the stern of thick boards. The heavy steel plate of the main deck served as the ceiling of the room. There were no portholes or other openings, no ventilation for fresh air, and light could enter only through the hatchway, which was kept covered except for the width of one plank along each side and a somewhat larger opening in the corner, where the head of the stairway was located. When it rained, as it frequently did in the tropics, even these openings had to be closed.

In passing across the deck from the gangway to the hatchway we had heard the guards refer to us as "the prisoners." The captain of the raider had said that we were his "guests." As we stood there in the hold of the *Dresden*, we began to realize that we were now to experience something of what it means to be "under hatches." Some of us recalled having read accounts of the miserable existence under hatches of the Africans, who were brought to America as slaves a century and more ago.

In our first survey of the room that was to be our dormitory for the next thirty-two nights, we had failed to observe that against one of the walls there was piled several bales of cotton. In another corner there was also a pile of mattresses, which we recognized as having come from the *Zamzam.* As we became accustomed to the semi-darkness of the room we discovered that there was not a stick of furniture, not even a bench.

In taking an inventory of the stack of mattresses we found that there were not half enough for our number. The mattresses were appropriated by those who were nearest to them. Those of us who were not fortunate enough to have secured one nor to have selected a location for themselves began to cast longing eyes on the bales of cotton, as the plank floor did look so hard and rough.

"All things come to him who waits," even in a situation like this. How grateful we were when we saw someone come down the stairway with an armful of narrow bags made of unbleached muslin. These were distributed to us and we set about to fill them with cotton. This was found to be a rather long and tedious process, as the pressed cotton had to be carefully fluffed. One had to keep adding to the contents of the bag from day to day until it attained a sufficient thickness. The planks on which our improvised mattresses were placed did not quite take the place of the comfortable bedsprings to which most Americans are accustomed. Another difficulty which some of us experienced was that they were of a uniform length, and not quite sufficient for six-footers. One way of solving that problem was to use the life preserver as an extension. Such an arrangement, in fact, proved to be most useful, as it gave us a sense of security to know that our head rest and pillow was near at hand, if in the darkness of the night we should find it necessary to make a hurried exit from the ship.

At 4:30 that first afternoon, while we were still busily engaged in our mattress making, some of the Egyptian stewards came down into the hold with dishpans of soup. Each one of us was provided with an enamel bowl, an aluminum cup and a soup spoon. With the soup we received a couple of pieces of brown bread and a cup of tea. That was our first meal on the *Dresden*. After the meal each one went to the deck above to wash his bowl, cup, and spoon at a hydrant drawing ocean water. It seemed so good to get away from our stuffy room in the hold for a while, so we lingered.

Fifteen minutes after sunset the guards ordered us down the hatch. It was quite dark down there, but one or two bright lights had been strung up, so we could find our way to our locations. These lights were very soon turned off, however, so we had barely enough time to get to our mattresses. We were relieved when later two rather dim lights were placed in the two far corners of the room. It was a rather interesting spectacle. There we were, strung out in rows, elbow to elbow, and covering most of the floor space. The lanes between the rows of locations were very narrow, indeed. If one ventured to travel from one location to another he had to be very careful not to be tripped by the feet of those who were of more than standard stature.

After an hour or so of chatting, and the singing of one or two songs, all became quiet. It had been another day of stress and strain, a day during which we had made our first adjustments to the unusual life we were to lead for the next few weeks. Some of us were unable to relax at once. How much we would have appreciated to be able to press the button of a bed lamp and reach for the Bible! But we remembered that both Bible and Testament had been lost in the waters of the Atlantic. Now, as many times before, we had occasion to thank God for our Christian heritage, for the family altar in our childhood home, for Sunday school and confirmation instruction, and for the liturgical worship of the church. It was so helpful to recall some of the precious words from the Book of Books that through the years had been stored away in our hearts. How reassuring it was to hear again the voice of the Master saying, "It is I. Be not afraid. Lo, I am with you always."

During the last days on the *Zamzam* some of us missionaries had been reading a recent book entitled "Out of the Night," a book painting a very lurid picture of present world conditions. We thanked God that in the present world darkness, the furious raging of the waves of class and national hatreds and suspicions, we still could hear the words of the Prince of Peace as he was walking the waters: "Be not afraid. . . . It is I. . . . I am with you." Indeed, had He not been with us on the yesterday as we passed through the waters, "a very present help in trouble"? Was He not even now making "a way in the sea, and a path in the mighty waters"? If He be with us, who could be against us? Even though we had been hindered on our way to the work to which we had been called, had He not given the assurance that the very gates of hell shall not prevail against the work of His church? Why should we doubt that He would somehow make these present adversities work together for the extension of His kingdom and for our good? With such thoughts we fell asleep.

At fifteen minutes before sunrise the guard called, "All out!" Wearied with twelve hours in the stuffy hold, we did not need to be called twice. We were eager and ready to come up into the fresh morning air at the earliest opportunity.

German raider *Tamesis* which shelled and sank the *Zamzam*. Photo by *Life* magazine.

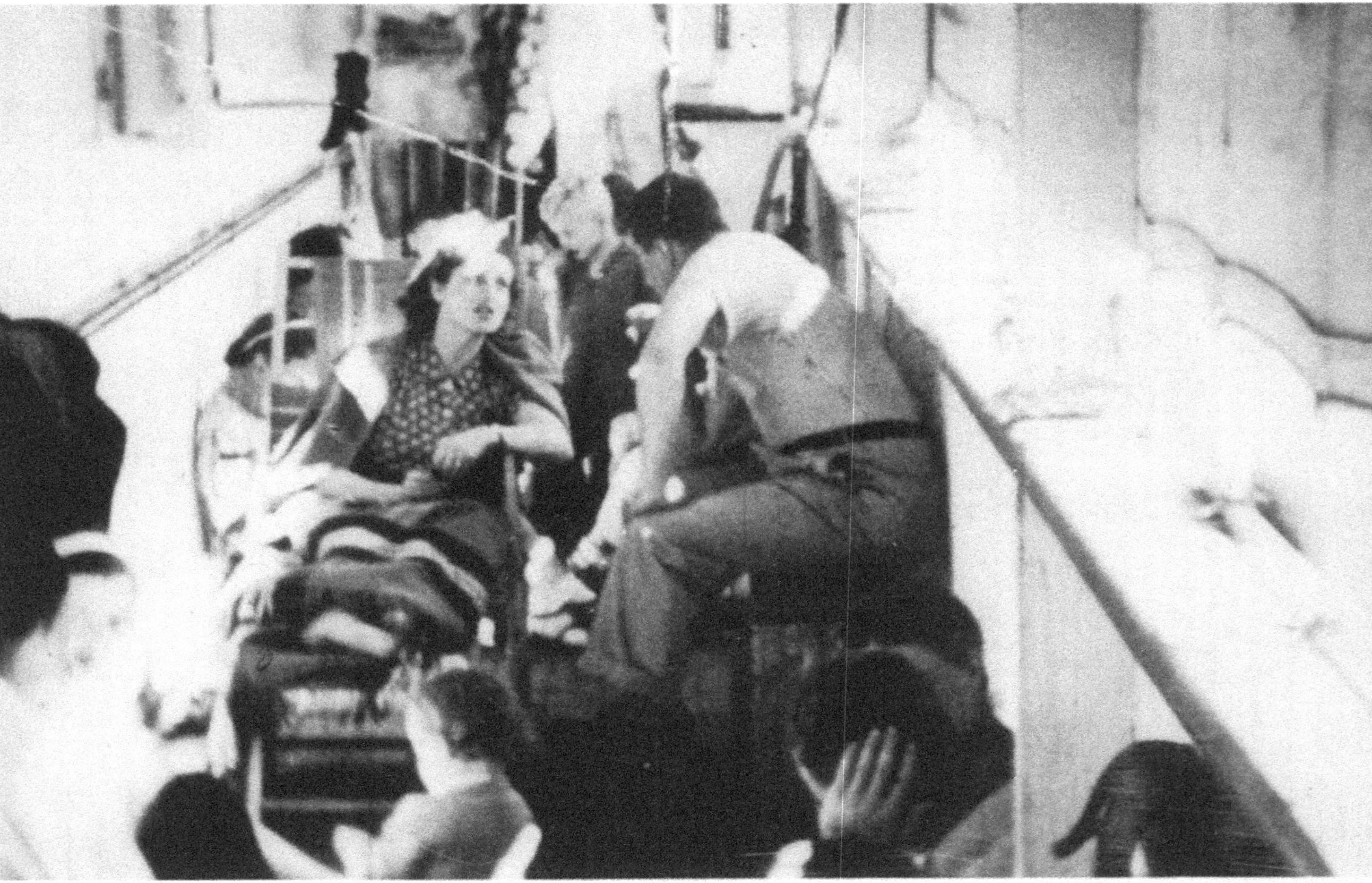

With our exit from the hold began the routine of the day. First there was the wash-up in a bucket containing a pint and a half of fresh water, the amount allotted to each man for the day. After the cleansing of the outer man as best we could with that precious bit of water the immediate needs of the inner man were to "break our fast" by eating a bowl of slightly sweetened, starchy gruel and a couple of slices of brown bread with a cup of tea. The meal was eaten picnic style on the deck or hatch.

That forenoon the captain paid us a visit. We were pleased to learn that he spoke English, so that he could address us directly. Though he spoke to us courteously, he did not seek to evade the fact that we were prisoners. He assured us that he knew what that meant, as he had himself been a prisoner for four years during the World War. He explained that as the captain of this ship he had a double responsibility. On the one hand he was under orders to make every effort to bring us safely to some neutral port, and on the other hand he must try to bring his ship safely to a home port. He assured us that, if we cooperated with him, he would do everything in his power and with the limited supplies and resources at his disposal, to make us as comfortable as possible. We were also given to understand that we might feel free to approach him at any reasonable time and occasion about any needs or problems that might arise. He stated that he did not know how long we would have to remain on his ship, but in rationing available supplies he would have to count on a month or more. It is needless to say that we appreciated this frankness on the part of him into whose hands our very lives had been laid. We were grateful to find the ship's officers, guards, and seamen considerate, and even courteous, at all times. We realized that, as prisoners of war, we might have fallen into the hands of a very different type of men.

At 12:30 noon the midday meal was served. It consisted of a bowl of thick soup with bits of meat cooked with evaporated vegetables and rice. With this we were also given the usual two slices of dark bread and a cup of tea. The captain assured us that he would see to it that space in lifeboats or on rafts would be provided for every man, woman, and child aboard his ship. The boats that had been salvaged from the *Zamzam* were being thoroughly inspected and overhauled. Preparations were also being made for the construction of a number of rafts. All life preservers were carefully inspected and numbered. All this was reassuring, because we realized that we were at all times in grave danger and might find it necessary at any hour of the day or night to leave the ship.

Again at 4:30 in the afternoon we saw the Egyptian stewards come out of the galley with dishpans of food. The menu for the evening meal was the same as on the day before. The ship's ping pong table was now put to use as a serving table. Six of the ambulance men served the food as we passed the table in two lines. Again there was the usual chore of washing and drying the dishes and of putting them away for the next meal. Some of us, who enjoy walking, spent the next hour or more pacing to and fro on the open space of the port side of the deck between the upper deck and the forecastle. Others stood about on the deck, quietly enjoying the sunset hour. All seemed bent on making the most of every minute, as they thought of soon being ordered down the hatch for the night.

Such was the life into which we entered when placed on the prison ship, a life of routine and yet not altogether uninteresting. No two days were quite the same in spite of the fact that out there in mid-ocean there is very little change of scenery. With more than two hundred men in the fore part of the ship, including the Egyptians and Sudanese, occupying the space of the hold under hatch No. 3 and the starboard side of the main deck, there was a most interesting variety of personalities. Within our own group of over one hundred, coming from many places and various walks of life in Europe, America, and even Africa, but now occupying one room, literally rubbing elbows during the hours of the day and sleeping elbow to elbow during the night, there was an unusually fine opportunity for close range study of human nature. It was very interesting to note, for instance, the various kinds of activity which were found or made. In spite of the fact that there were so few books available, as most of our books had gone down with the ship, it was surprising to find so many reading. One book would be passed between several persons in the course of one day. This was particularly true of books of devotion and theology. Among the missionaries quite a number had saved their Bibles or Testaments. Among the most treasured memories the writer has of those days are those of seeing individuals on the deck and in the hold pouring over the open Bible, or of groups, seated on a hatch, listening to one of their number as he read from the Book. Not much writing was done for the simple reason that it seemed quite probable that records and writings of any kind would be subject to censorship and confiscation. It was surprising to see what could be done with only an ordinary pocketknife and a board, a block, or even a stick. If all the things thus made during these weeks could be assembled, it would be a most interesting exhibit, revealing the resourcefulness of the human hand and mind. With nothing but a few boards, some pieces of burlap, and a few tools a shower bath and booth was built on the deck. The daily use of this shower and occasional use of the ship's tiled swimming pool on the officers' deck, were a real boon to us.

On the fourth day after being placed on the prison ship we were gladdened by the news that the room on the port side of the forecastle had been cleared and might be used as a place for our daily devotional meetings. At other hours of the day it might be used as a social room. With that room are associated some very helpful memories. These devotional meetings were informal. It was to be expected that they would be attended mainly by the missionaries, but there were others who came in occasionally. Though the missionaries of the group had been commissioned by about twenty boards, representing various shades of religious faith and varying missionary practices, these "assemblings together" seemed to mean much to all who took part in them. These daily meetings "beside the still waters" and in "the green pastures" of God's Word helped us to a clearer recognition of what are the fundamentals of the Christian faith, what all true followers of the Christ have in common. One of the favorite hymn verses sung at these gatherings was:

"Blest be the tie that binds
Our hearts in Christian love:
The fellowship of kindred minds
Is like to that above."

LIFE OF THE WOMEN ABOARD THE PRISON SHIP

MRS. C. EINAR NORBERG

We are pressed on every side, yet not straitened; perplexed, yet not unto despair.
2 Corinthians 4. 8.

After the wounded had been transferred from the *Tamesis* to the prison ship, the women and children were the next to go. Ready to direct us as we came up on the deck of the *Dresden* was Captain Jaeger himself. He had a list of the names of the *Zamzam* women and children in his hands.

"Mrs. Norberg, this is your cabin. You will have to have someone else in with you. Do you have a preference as to whom you would have?"

It was a lovely cabin for two. There were two good spring beds. But when all the women and children were at last housed, we found that we were nine in our two-bed cabin! There was no fresh running water coming through the taps. Instead we were issued one liter of water per person morning and evening. Our clothes we washed in salt water.

The chief steward showed us where we would have our meals. Temporary tables, made of long planks, had been placed in the space cleared by the removal of the permanent tables.

Uppermost in our minds was the query, what has become of the men? Were they to remain on the *Tamesis*, or had they, too, been transferred to this ship? A group of our young boys soon gave us the answer. Each one as he saw his father would exclaim, "I saw my Daddy come up the gangplank." The men were all sent forward into hatch No. 2. Again we wondered what kind of accommodations they could have under hatch No. 2. Were they all on board this ship or had some of them been detained on the *Tamesis?* The whole atmosphere on this ship emphasized our status as prisoners.

Five o'clock in the afternoon, and we had already had the evening meal of soup, sour bread, and practically tealess tea! We went out on deck. A young missionary wife was leaning on the ship's rail, looking out over the vast sea. She chanced to look toward the front of the ship. She gave a shout of joy. There she spied the heads of several of our men as they, too, were looking out over the watery world about us. Each one of the ladies took her turn to stand in the most advantageous place to wave to the men on the foredeck. The men co-operated nobly by calling the husband to the railing to acknowledge his wife's greeting. One of the German guards smiled at us. I ventured to ask if he or one of the other guards would please take a few notes over to our husbands. We wanted to relieve them of any undue anxiety over our welfare. This guard, a friendly fellow, said he would gladly do that. I asked him, "When?" "Jetz," was his answer. And he did.

For these notes of courage and comfort we used any odd bits of paper we had in our possession. We had not talked to our husbands for two days; therefore these notes meant much to us. But alert Captain Jaeger soon noticed the elation among the men and women as they stood in small groups reading the love messages.

"What kind of foolishness is this?" was his question. "This must be stopped!"

And stop it did. His heart, however, softened, and he gave the men having families on board the privilege of spending the two hours from ten to twelve each forenoon with their wives and children. The unattached men were later given the same privilege. But due to the limited space allowed on the deck for these visits only six of them were permitted on the women's side each day.

These visiting hours were spent on the very narrow promenade decks. The doors leading to all corridors were locked and an armed guard stood watch. Here the small family groups would sit on the floor, through the heat of the equator climate, as well as in rains and the cold winds of the North Atlantic. There was very little privacy possible, but we did have our daily family devotions together. We could speak words of comfort and cheer to each other. How thankful we felt each time we could sit as a family, five in a row!

It was hard to hear the guard announce, "Visiting time is up." Each day as I saw my husband walk down the steps and turn the corner leading forward I would think, "Will I see him again?" This was particularly true the week we ran the British blockade.

These hours were always the brightest and most eagerly looked forward to of each day.

The first nine days on the *Dresden* we marked time. We would sail at full speed a few hours and then circle right back. At times we were simply idling away time on the rolling sea. Captain Jaeger was to receive final orders from the commander of the *Tamesis.* We were waiting for that ship to make its appearance again. At last the *Tamesis* did come into view.

Three of the most seriously wounded had been left on board this ship. The wife of one of them, as well as representatives from the tobacco buyers and from the ambulance corps, were allowed to go over to visit the three men. They brought back reports that two were recovering nicely, but the third was not so well.

We saw the sailors putting crate after crate of Brazilian eggs on our boat. At least we would have eggs to vary our steady diet of soup, soup, noon and night.

Officials assured us we would not run the British blockade. Captain Jaeger was to get back into the regular trade lane. There he would try to get us transferred to a neutral ship. If that failed he would bring us into a neutral South American port.

Days passed by. The officers on the bridge may have known about ships in our vicinity, but we did not see any sign of a neutral ship the first two or three weeks. We had already gone too far north to believe we would ever be taken to a South American port. Word came out we were to go to Tenerife in the Canary Island group.

Some doubted the validity of this report. They felt certain that we would now be brought into occupied France. We made plans as to what we would do just in case the Tenerife report should prove true. One missionary had a copy of the *East African Handbook.* We figured out overland routes to take to our desired destination from the valuable information found in this book. We, the Augustana folks, would have to go by Portuguese ship down to Lobito Bay on the West Coast of Africa. From there we would begin the long trip across Africa. It would be a trying trip, as we would have to start without equipment, but we would be on our way back to Africa.

These hopes grew fainter as our course took us farther into the North Atlantic. Now it became more and more certain that that which we had dreaded most was to happen. We were to run the British blockade.

Our first day on board the *Dresden* Captain Jaeger told me, "You'll not be on this ship over forty days." He mentioned something about weighing the children once a week.

Forty days! I had hoped it would be but three or four days or a week at the very most. It seemed best to settle down to a routine life. This we ourselves would have to make as pleasant and profitable as we could.

As soon as we were allowed to get at the odd pieces of baggage which the German sailors had rescued from our *Zamzam* cabins, we tried to see that everyone had clothes enough to be properly dressed. There were women who had gone barefoot for three days. Some were still wearing night apparel or housecoats. Many of the children were meagerly dressed. Most of those who had some clothing to spare were quite willing to share with the less fortunate, and before many days had passed we were all properly clothed, though not in the latest fashion.

Captain Jaeger gave us a large bolt of very course unbleached muslin. We were to sew anything we needed. The privilege to use the ship's sewing machine was well appreciated. We started by sewing extensions to the men's mattresses. Cases for cotton pillows were made. The women made bags of every size and description. We were not to be caught unprepared a second time. Our most precious belongings, salvaged from the lot brought off the *Zamzam*, were placed in the bags which could be carried from the shoulders by straps. Swimming trunks for the men were fabricated. The swimming pool was cleansed and filled to be used during the hottest days while we were in the neighborhood of the equator. Married men, single men, women and children each had their specified time for the cooling off.

Every inch of wool yarn or crochet thread found in any suitcase was worked up. We had to keep busy.

There were thirty-six children on board. Sixteen of them were of school age. Almost every day the children received a small cookie or two, or a small square of German chocolate after the noon and evening meals. A committee of women supervised the distribution of these titbits. These were handed to the children after they had eaten their bowl of soup, not before.

We tried having the children do some school work. This was not so easy. Their minds were not at ease and their surroundings far from inducive to studying. But our faithful teachers gathered this little missionary band each morning for prayer and singing. Often we heard them singing, "My cup is full and running over."

The children found ways of passing the time. Hide-and-seek was even there the stand-by. Checkerboards were made out of cardboard they got from the chief steward or a guard. Mothers' button boxes were all gone, so they had to make cardboard checkers. The wind had a way of carrying these off to sea. The daddies up on the foredeck made Chinese-checker boards. Wooden pegs were used instead of marbles. The older boys took to wood carving. The girls begged Mother for knitting needles. Most of the time the children kept in good spirit.

Several children celebrated their birthdays on the *Dresden*. An English mother had a couple packages of American jello in her bag. When her little daughter's birthday came around, it took the place of both cake and dessert. For other birthday parties the children would save their cookies, received after the noon meal, to be eaten at the afternoon party.

Mothers, too, have birthdays. We, the five Augustana women on board the *Dresden*, will long remember the day we celebrated Mrs. Danielson's birthday. We had no cookies to carry with us to the party, even though we had eaten our bowl of soup nicely. Our teachers came to our rescue. They had a very small tube of powdered coffee. It was enough for one good cup of coffee. It had to be thinned out to make five cups for this occasion. It had at least one resemblance to coffee—it was hot. It was served in our tin cups. The birthday cake was pieces of the sour, dark bread gleaned from our noon meal. We tried to celebrate the birthday of our dear friend in good spirits at least.

Our *Dresden* days gave us hours of deep anxiety and worry. But there were hours of joy as well. "We are pressed on every side, yet not straitened; perplexed, yet not unto despair." 2 Cor. 4. 8. Many were the times we sang "Safe am I, safe am I in the hollow of thy hand," and "God will take care of you." Precious to us all were the hours of Christian fellowship and prayer. In our own strength we were helpless, but we knew upon whom to call. Our Father never turns a deaf ear to them that call upon Him in sincerity. Nine-fifteen each morning found us gathered up on deck for morning prayers. We shared with each other the many promises of comfort and cheer found in God's Word. "Who delivered us out of so great a death, and will deliver: on whom we have set our hope that he will also still deliver us," 2 Cor. 1. 10, is a promise one of our African Inland Mission ladies called to our attention. She is today in a German concentration camp. May she and others of our *Zamzam* friends with her, daily claim this promise.

In the evenings we met in smaller groups in the cabins, the doors to the deck having been locked fifteen minutes after sunset. It was so sweet to place ourselves in His tender care and keeping for the hours of another night at sea.

Then we had the sweetness of the children's evening prayers. Besides our three were two little Jewish children in the cabin. During the shelling of the *Zamzam* their mother had had both feet seriously cut by shrapnel. Miss Olson and Miss Kinnan had taken complete charge of these little ones. Peter was eight and Wendy three years of age.

Peter loved to hear the stories about Jesus. These were true and beautiful stories! His place was always next to the person reading. And little Wendy, she could sing "Jesus loves me, Jesus loves me." Today little Peter and Wendy together with their mother are in a German concentration camp. May they there remember that Jesus loves them.

RUNNING THE BRITISH BLOCKADE

C. EINAR NORBERG

And now I exhort you to be of good cheer; for there shall be no loss of life among you, but only of the ship.
Acts 27. 22.

The uncertainty of our destination was beginning to fray the nerves of the men in hatch No. 2. Another night in the hold had passed without mishap to the ship. The promise of a new day of grace was given us with the first faint glimmer of daylight finding its way down into the hold and there revealing quite a number of men already filling the limited space around the ladder leading up to fresh air. Only one man at a time had permission to leave the hold during the night. In the morning the officer on the bridge decided when it was safe to turn us all loose. We had been duly informed that all rules must be implicitly obeyed lest there should be any unfortunate accident. An armed guard was pacing back and forth all night on the iron deck above us.

"Which way are we heading this morning?" was the question directed to a man who had just returned to the hold from an early visit on deck.

"Still pointing her nose to the North Pole, and it is plenty chilly up there this morning," was his answer. It was going on seventeen days we had kept the same course, so a change would be news.

Now and then an impatient muttering was heard from some one in the crowded stairway about this useless prolongation of the long night confinement. Daylight was steadily pushing the dark shadows of night farther into the less accessible corners of the hold. Finally the officer in charge on the bridge shouted to the weary guard on the foredeck that the "gefangene" were now permitted on top.

There was a rush up the stairway and a scramble for the four or five galvanized buckets. Others hurried to the forecastle where they could get their cigarettes lit at an electric contrivance rigged up for that purpose, matches being on the "verboten" list. A few made for the cold shower bath, which had been such a boon to us in the warmer climate. A German sailor stood by the tub of fresh water and measured out to each man his allotted one liter of water for his daily ablution, shave, and sponge bath. Those who failed to get a pail, and most of them did, had to get their water in their enameled soup bowl. The inherent sense of sanitary necessity had to be greatly subdued.

May 13 was a regular day for us on the North Atlantic, except that this day we had a brand new rumor adrift among us. The news had originated on the women's side of the ship that we were to change course at noon. Surprisingly enough that rumor proved to be true. At 12 o'clock we turned east.

We had hoped against all fears that we would not have to pass the British blockade of the European continent on a German ship. We knew now that the promises of the long days passed were not true. It became increasingly evident that our destination would be an occupied French port. The horrible reality of another sea battle as one-sided as the one we lived to witness on the *Zamzam* was not difficult to visualize. In fact it seemed more probable than improbable. Captain Jaeger had promised not to resist a British warship. In case of an encounter he would signal the information that he carried 300 noncombatants on his ship. We, however, felt that this promise could not be rated much higher than some of the other empty promises we had seen so confidently disregarded. We had seen him turn his ship around and flee on several occasions whenever the smoke from another vessel appeared over the horizon.

The unanswered questions in our minds were: How long would he attempt to get away in case of a pursuit? Would he stop before his ship was seriously crippled? He had also assured us that the British would never take his ship. He could blow it up by throwing a switch on the bridge. His temperament seemed in perfect agreement with that type of action. We had seen sailors put up a strong barricade around the bridge. Bales of hemp, heavy boards, and sand bags had been piled up to protect the men on the bridge. All such preparation did not indicate that the Germans intended to give up without a struggle.

The very careful lookout the Germans kept over the sea from the day we fell into their hands really merited our admiration. An even more diligent watch was now kept over the distant horizon all around us. Whatever happened they were not likely to be caught unawares.

We were told that from now until we would land we must sleep fully dressed and with the life jacket always near at hand. It was not difficult to obey this command because by this time we were in an area of the Atlantic where it was cold and we needed all the clothes we could muster for our protection. The life jacket was a precious possession which no one despised. It served nicely as a pillow at night and as a soft seat when we were on deck. Each individual had his or her number stenciled on the life jacket so it would be difficult to claim your neighbor's jacket in case your own was lost.

The most likely attack at night would be by a submarine launching a torpedo at us, and that, we were assured, would come without warning. The German and Italian submarines would be informed of our whereabouts, but the officers could not promise anything about the actions of the British submarines. We were also instructed how to take cover in case a bombing plane came over us. According to Captain Jaeger a plane pilot of either side who would see a group of women and children on the decks would hold his fire, but occasionally there is an idiot in one of those planes who seems to delight in opening up on just such a target. If the captain had any personal experience with such an individual he did not say, but his advice to take cover was well received. A simple set of signals were explained to us whereby we might know what particular type of danger we were confronting.

Lifeboat drills became more frequent, and the captain took particular care that we should get out of the hold within one minute. Two extra-wide rope ladders were hung down into the hold to facilitate a hasty evacuation. We were told repeatedly that there would not be much time to clear out in case of an attack upon us. We could easily imagine what would happen in case a torpedo hit our hold. The only two lifeboats which the Germans saw fit to salvage from the *Zamzam* wrecks were repaired and hoisted up on special scaffolds with rope and tackles so that they could be launched by man power should the electric power of the ship fail us at the critical moment. The captain himself supervised all lifeboat drills, and he went the entire round each time.

Permission was now granted us to keep two of our own group as guards on the hatch at night. They were to assist in opening the hatch in case of need and to help get the men out. The Germans exercised meticulous care, but whatever they did it was always done with the same supreme confidence.

These were days and long nights of anxious care to those of us in particular who had loved ones in another part of the ship. We knew we could not expect to be of any assist-

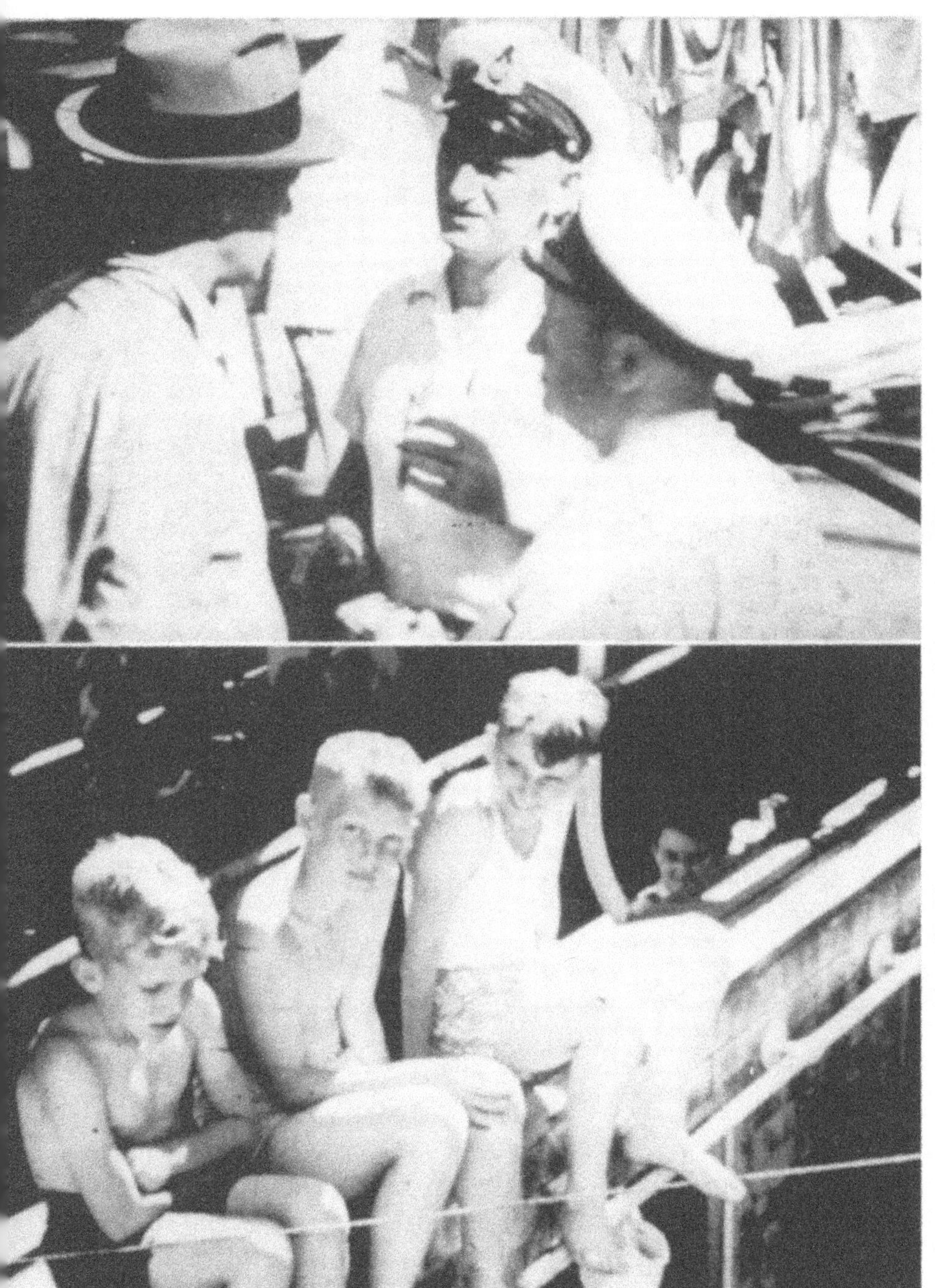

(1) Mr. Chas. Murphy of *Fortune* magazine. Capt. Jaeger (center) of the *Dresden*. Capt. Smith of the *Zamzam*. (2) Carl Norberg, Lawrence Danielson and Robert Buyse aboard the *Dresden*. Photos by V. Eugene Johnson.

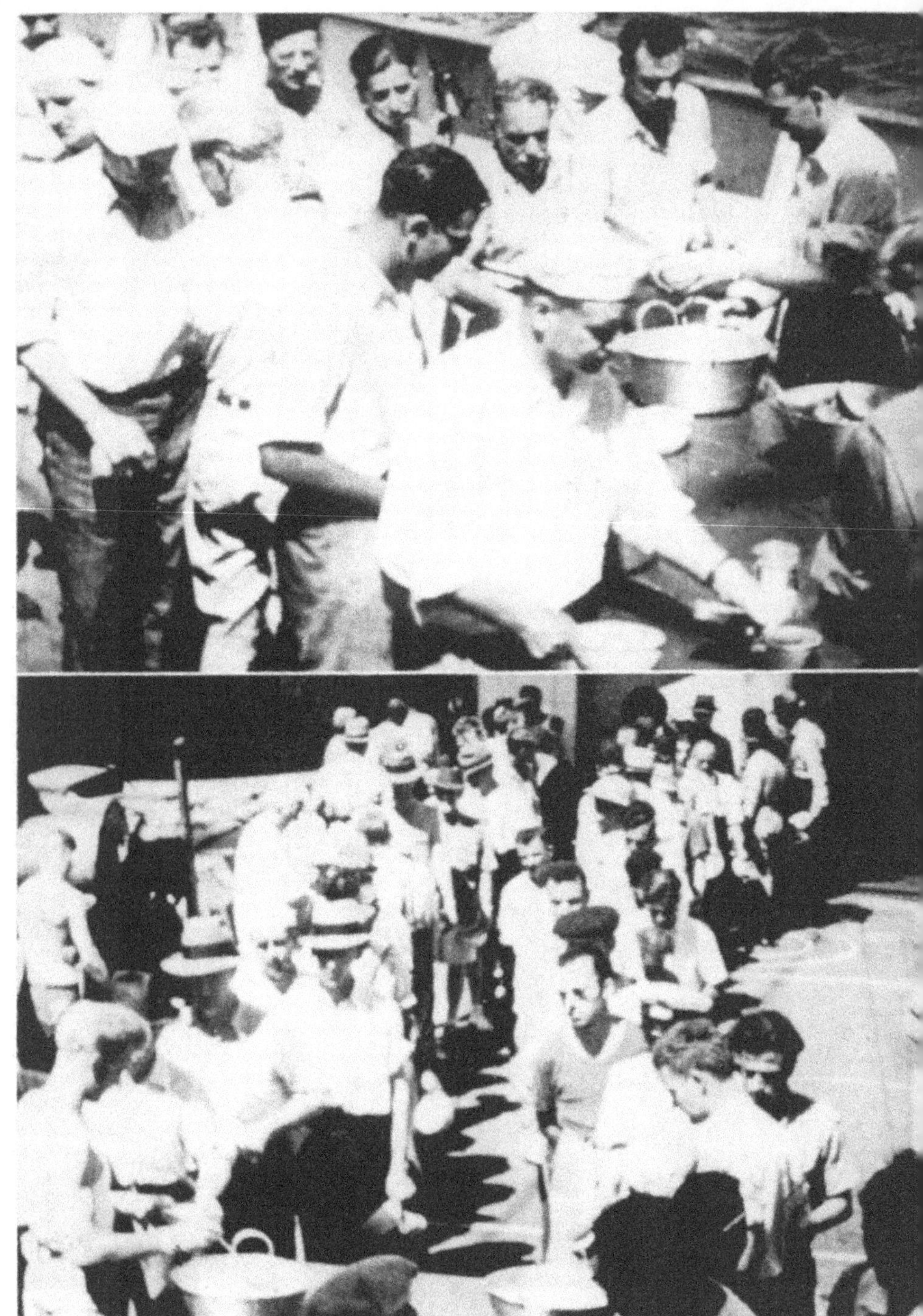

Mealtime on the *Dresden*. Tin cups used for all purposes. Photos by V. Eugene Johnso

ance to them in case we should be subjected to another shelling by a warship. We had no means of appealing to any *men* for help. True, we were citizens of a mighty nation, but we could not get word to the men in authority of that nation. The prison ship carried a complete wireless equipment, but it was not placed at our disposal. But we did send many and frequent wireless messages to Him who still has all authority in heaven and on earth. Not even the military power in whose hands we were could stop us from sending those messages. We had the spiritual satisfaction of throwing all our problems before the Lord in prayer. We met as a group twice each day, and we noticed that a few who had not previously attended our prayer sessions came reverently and sat in with us as we waited upon the Lord. On one of the last Sundays on this prison ship at morning worship we heard a message from one of the missionaries on the topic: "Have Faith in God." How appropriate and how comforting it is to be reminded that we have a living Lord who looks after his own even in the dark valley.

"The darkness deepens; Lord with me abide!
When other helpers fail, and comforts flee,
Help of the helpless, O abide with me."

He received and answered our messages. One of the business men said after we arrived in France: "Captain Jaeger may attribute his success in bringing us safely to port to his luck, but as for me I am convinced the Lord answered the prayers of the missionaries." Yes, we also saw the hand of the Lord in his dealings with us. We had not been on our course eastward long before we ran into stormy weather. We had not prayed for a storm. No, on the other hand, we were much perturbed as we beheld the rising waves and the bitterly cold wind with the rain and the mist narrowing down our little world. How hard it would be to take to the lifeboats in such a turbulent sea! Later we learned that it would have been nigh impossible for a submarine to operate against us in such a sea. The visibility for efficient airplane scouting was at its worst in such misty weather. The Lord most likely had something to do about it.

The captain now ceased coming down to the foredeck for his customary chats. He was busy on the bridge, where he spent most of his time, day and night. There may have been another reason for his nonappearance among us. He could not well have escaped understanding our keen disappointment over his apparent intention of taking us through the dangerous waters to a belligerent port in Europe contrary to his promises. He always justified his position by stating that he had to obey the orders of his superiors whenever one of his promises were obviously disregarded. We had our suspicions now that there had never been any change in the orders. Those false promises of being set ashore on a neutral island or on a neutral ship were given out simply to keep us in better humor on the long trip to France. In war human life is not the most important item. Military objectives and advantages of position come first. To get the *Dresden* to a home port safely was the prime objective in this case. The nuisance of 332 civilians on board was something to be tolerated, but could under no circumstances take on such importance as to swerve them from their objective.

A number of passengers still clung to the hope that we would be put off at a Portuguese or Spanish port. It made a great difference to our friends of other nationalities, such as the Canadians, British, Greeks, Belgians, and Egyptians, whether we went to a German-occupied port or to a neutral port. It was either freedom or the lot of a prisoner for the duration of the war. Even to us Americans it seemed much more desirable to be placed in a neutral port. Such good fortune was not to be expected.

On Sunday, May 18, we received the news from the captain that land would be sighted within twenty-four hours. The long dreadful suspense was actually drawing to a close! We had not seen land since we left Brazil on April 10. Many of us had never been on water that long before, and none of us had ever tried it under such trying conditions. What a comfortable feeling it would be to see green grass, trees, and even bare rocks once more. At one o'clock that afternoon the ship turned around and started retracing its steps. This time, however, we could see no sign of any approaching ship. To us there was no visible explanation for this strange action. True to human curiosity such a happening could not be left without a plausible explanation. The wiser members of our party did not delay long in offering a workable hypothesis. The ship had traveled faster than had been expected of it, and as this would upset the schedule of our arrival, we had to waste the time at sea. It would be very dangerous to stay still in this particular part of the ocean, so a retracing of our course would be more feasible. This assumption was not universally accepted. Whatever the reason for this strange maneuver the ship was turned back to its eastern course after two hours of waywardness, and everyone felt much better.

A Welcome Light at Night

Shortly after sunset that same day while getting our last fill of fresh air on deck before the inevitable order to get down into the hold, we noticed a faint flicker of light on the horizon ahead from our starboard side. After examining it more intently we decided it must be a signal of some kind. It came at regular intervals and from the very same spot. Could it possibly be a lighthouse! More people were called to verify our hopes and before long the entire group was staring at this strange phenomena. The captain on the bridge, who had previously been notified about the lighthouse by his lookout in the crow's nest, called down to us and said: "What is all the excitement about below? Did I not tell you we would see land within twenty-four hours?" He was implying we should have harbored no doubts about his veracity.

The feeling we experienced in seeing this lighthouse is indescribable. We asked the captain if the women, who had already been locked up for the night, could not be notified about this happy turn of events. This was granted, and all of us rested with much less anxiety than had been our lot for many nights. Prayers of thanksgiving and praise ascended to the Almighty from this prison ship that night.

WE ARRIVE IN FRANCE

EDYTHE J. JOHNSON

Thou didst cause men to ride over our heads;
We went through fire and through water;
But thou broughtest us out into a wealthy place.
Psalm 66. 12.

On May 19, 1941, which some have designated as Black Monday because they learned that day that the *Zamzam* had been sunk, its passengers and crew, who had been rescued from a watery grave, were still aboard the prison ship. It was just then completing the long voyage from Capetown, and was running the British blockade. Were you one of the thousands of friends who prayed for the safety of both passengers and crew? God answered your prayer. In the evening we saw the lights of Finisterre, and the next day we were escorted by three destroyers to St. Jean-de-Luz.

Seventy long days had passed since we bade farewell to loved ones in Minneapolis and vicinity. After two trying months of sea travel we were eager to set our feet on land. Our few possessions were excitedly packed before daylight so that we could be free to view the picturesque French town at which we were to disembark. Perhaps we embarrassed the German sailors of three mine sweepers by watching their attempt to get the grounded *Dresden* off a sand bar.

The attractive seaside resort of St. Jean-de-Luz seemed entirely deserted in the early gray morning. Later we saw a company of German soldiers march to their barracks. Then a truck rumbled heavily along the highway. We wanted to know more about this place, so we tried to secure information from two of the passengers who had visited the town. As usual we were kept in ignorance of our next move, so we could make no plans except to trust the Lord moment by moment that He would direct us to the place of His choosing. The children talked about the castles they would build in the sand, the flowers they would pluck, and about the races they would run as soon as their feet touched land.

The joy of landing was, however, to be mingled with sorrow. About midafternoon the passengers traveling on American passports were shocked to learn that all other members of the passengers and crew would be kept on the *Dresden* and taken to Bordeaux. We pleaded with the officers, but we could not secure the release of our dear friends. Our hearts sorrowed as we saw husbands separated from their wives. We could scarcely say good-by to our dear co-workers in the Lord and other friends. The children could not understand why only twenty-eight of their group had permission to leave the *Dresden*.

"Why do they have to remain prisoners?" my older son asked.

We descended the gangplank, waved a sad farewell, and were quickly transported to the docks. Behind the large, imposing hotels, which stood like silent sentinels along the deserted seaside, we found hundreds of sad-faced French people living under the iron heel of their oppressors. We were wards of the German Navy and guests of the German Red Cross. The *Dresden* had arrived one day sooner than expected, which necessitated a rush to empty three hotels of their occupants, in order that our group of one hundred and seventeen could be kept together as one prison group. We rode in buses from St. Jean-de-Luz via Bayonne to Biarritz.

The once gay playground of kings and princes of Europe did not present a happy picture. For two days we were confined to our hotels and the street just outside. Though we found a good air-raid shelter near our hotel, we did not have to make use of it. Food was scarce even in that favored corner of Europe. About eleven o'clock that first evening we were called to supper. A complete blackout was observed, so we groped our way down seven flights of steps, then across a narrow street to the dining hall, where we feasted on bread, butter, sausage, and coffee. It was good to sit together again as a family at a small table, and to praise the Lord for His mercy to the children of men. The children were almost asleep before we groped through the rain and blackness up to our hotel again.

The German authorities warned us against conversing with the townspeople. The first time I opened our New Testament in the hotel room my eye was caught by the command in Acts 18. 9–10, "Be not afraid, but speak and hold not thy peace: for I am with thee, and no man shall set on thee to harm thee: for I have much people in this city." Knowing that we ought to obey God rather than men, I decided to comfort others with the same word of God by which we had been comforted as God placed opportunities before us.

More than once I saw hungry children and old people rummage in the garbage cans behind the hotels in which the German soldiers were living. I saw no wasted scraps in any other section. There was the usual scarcity of men so noticeable to strangers in war-torn countries. Hundreds of older adults and children wore mourning bands. There were no smiling faces and no songs among the French people. A spirit of sadness pervaded the land. No public meetings were advertised. All the news was censored, as well as the mail.

Only the conquerors sang as they marched with their hobnailed shoes or boots resounding through the streets. The natural beauty with which God clothes His creation healed our wounded hearts. After many weary hours spent in interviewing the authorities, we were finally granted exit visas to Spain and Portugal. We had been interviewed by the Gestapo police, who posed as journalists. Our movements had been carefully watched, and our every word carefully weighed. Freedom held a new meaning for us.

Again we made ready to move and packed our little cases carefully. Our joy was greatly decreased when we learned that twenty-two American ambulance boys, in the noncombatant service, were to remain prisoners. The French people sent warmest greetings to America as we departed in buses. We were escorted to Spanish soil by representatives of the United States embassy in Madrid. Truly a wonderful Memorial Day came to us Americans on May 30, when we were released from German domination, and turned our eyes toward the freedom and joy which awaited us in our beloved homeland.

IN SPAIN AND PORTUGAL

ESTHER M. OLSON

He will deliver thee in six troubles; yea, in seven there shall no evil touch thee. Job 5. 19.

On Friday evening, May 30, Velura and I came back from a walk to a French cemetery in Biarritz. The others had good news for us.

"Be ready before nine in the morning," they said, "for the Germans are sending buses to take us to the Spanish border."

We were thrilled at their words. Soon we would be free! We would be able to send messages to our dear ones. We would, no doubt, soon be on our way to Africa.

Hendaye, France, was reached on Saturday morning after a short bus ride. From there we traveled by train to San Sebastian, Spain. Large open Red Cross trucks met us at the depot. Reporters and photographers swarmed around us. For the first time in months we heard news of the world.

The beautiful hotel, the Maria Christina, was to be our home that first afternoon of freedom. As we rode down the San Sebastian streets we stared with nearly unbelieving eyes at all we saw. Here we were in Spain, we who had started for Africa.

The entire fourth floor of the hotel had been allowed for our use. Such elegance after prison ships and France! Dinner was served in the spacious dining room, soup, fish, meat, potatoes, custard. Oh, so good! Already the white enamel bowls and tin cups seemed remote.

Resting and sightseeing occupied the afternoon, and in the early evening we boarded the train for Lisbon. Cars had been reserved for us all and everything was done for our comfort. During the night, coaches were changed, and when all were settled again, several of us had no places to sit. The young assistant from the consul's office who was traveling with us and helping in every possible way took us up to a coach far ahead in the train. We passed through car after car, packed with Spanish people, sitting as closely as they could on the seats and on the floor, standing up in the aisles and on the platforms. Everywhere they were. We were told that many people in Spain carry their few belongings on their backs and go this way from place to place. Third-class railroad tickets are cheap, and they ride from one town to another, begging or working a few days and then going on again.

Our Saturday supper and Sunday breakfast had been packed in individual lunch boxes by the good friends in San Sebastian. The whole-wheat rolls, which we ate with such relish, had been baked in the kitchen of the American ambassador's home. The flour had been left from a shipment by the American Red Cross to Spain during the Civil War there.

As we went through one town after the other, nestled there on the hillsides, we saw children and older people at the depots, touching their mouths and then holding their empty hands out to us in a most beseeching way. Their thin faces and bodies showed plainly the lack of food. We had been warned against spending in Spain. They did not need American money, but they did need every bit of food they had.

Poor Spain! The damage done by bombing in their late conflict had not yet been repaired. They seemed to lack both funds and spirit for this needed reconstruction.

On and up we went into the night. It was good to see

lighted windows in the homes we passed, good to be away from the blackouts in occupied France.

Sunday, June first. Pentecost Day.

We spent it in a crowded compartment of a Spanish train. We read again the glorious birthday story of the Christian Church and asked God to fill us with His Spirit that we might be used to His honor.

Our noon meal was eaten at a railroad station restaurant. The wood-burning locomotive made remarkably good time, and soon we were in Portugal.

New sights kept us at the windows. Olive orchards, vineyards, herds of bulls, carefully terraced plots (not a bit of precious land could be wasted), groups of staring people at the stations—it was all so fascinatingly strange.

At about eight o'clock the train slowed down, and we were at the little town of Mangualde. So many were at the station, it seemed that the entire community had turned out to greet the Americans. And such a greeting!

A long table had been placed on the platform. It was laden with roses, strawberries, cherries, sponge cakes, and just as the train stopped the last dishes were filled with steaming soup. We could hardly believe our eyes. This was true Portuguese hospitality and what a good time they had serving us. The townspeople stood as close as they dared, little folks, big folks, their smiles of welcome told us all they could not say in words.

Such delicious food, course after course—but what was best of all, their joy at being able to do this for us. Pentecost Day, 1941. Who of us will ever forget that day!

After we had eaten, Mrs. Muir, a missionary from Portuguese East Africa, thanked them in Portuguese for all of us, and then there were shouts of "Long live America!" and "Long live Portugal!" In too short a time we had to go back to the train, and as it pulled slowly away we waved our thanks and smiled through grateful tears to these new, kind friends.

The next morning we reached Lisbon and rode in buses to Sintra, a gemlike little place twenty miles outside the capital city.

Now we were guests of the American Red Cross. We were given comfortable rooms in hotels, and such delicious food! White bread, potatoes, fruit, as much of everything as we could eat. Roses blooming in riotous profusion everywhere. Windows were lighted at night and seemed to speak quietly of peace and security. There was singing, there was laughter, there was beauty on every hand. Lovely little Portugal!

Every effort was made to secure passage from Lisbon to Africa. One day a cable from our State Department ordered the *Zamzam* survivors to return to America. When the Government orders, American citizens obey. We were keenly disappointed. We had wanted so much to go to Africa.

It was very unlikely that we would ever be in Portugal again, so we tried to see as much as we possibly could.

We tramped up to the Pena Palace where the king spent his last night in Portugal, and explored the Moorish fortifications built to protect the palace from the invaders. At the exquisitely beautiful Monserrate Gardens we found trees and plants from every part of the world. We picked cork off trees, that surpassed our wildest dreams. In ultra-modern Estaril, the Portuguese exposition and the president's home were most interesting sights.

One Monday we visited a Roman Catholic Academy, a private school and a public school. At the latter we were surprised to see the children stand and salute us. Then they sang, with spirit and strength. Each child pays a tuition fee of about eight cents per week. We saw some outside who lacked the needed coins, and their indifference at not being able to get in was a strange contrast to our American children who come running to school, all eager to get there on time.

Lisbon, the largest open port in Europe, was a busy cosmopolitan city. To see outlying parts of it, we would ride street cars to the end of the line and then back again. When we passed their elaborate building projects, it was easy to imagine ourselves in America.

We had heard of the Lisbon Art Gallery and were dismayed to find it closed the afternoon we went to visit. But when the director heard that we were Americans from the ill-fated *Zamzam*, the museum was opened and Velura and I enjoyed to the full our privately escorted tour.

On Sunday, June 8, we had Sunday school on the veranda of one of the hotels, and after that a service in the living room. As a group of missionaries we had had many services together. This was our last, for on Tuesday, the twenty-six "unattached ones" were to go to Lisbon to board a ship for America.

That afternoon our Augustana Synod "Nineteen" had our last coffee together and strengthened with pleasant fellowship the hands of love which had been made strong through common suffering and still stronger as we rejoiced over God's wonderful deliverance. And now, when the time of separation was near, it was good to remember that hitherto the Lord had helped us and no matter what the future held we could be assured of the guidance of our Saviour, who had promised to be with us always.

HOMEWARD BOUND

VELURA KINNAN

"So it's home again and home again,
America for me."

So he bringeth them unto their desired haven.
Psalm 107. 30.

In these lines there is a note of expectancy and joy to the adventurer who has saturated and satisfied himself with the glories of the old world, but to the missionary whose face is set toward Africa and whose heart is bent upon the "business of the King," they have a different ring. They were orders from the State Department that defeated our purpose. There was no alternative. We must obey.

With heavy hearts we began to fold and pack the few belongings we had saved. As we worked our minds questioned.

Why had our plans for service come to naught?

Were we not within God's will?

Had we not prayed enough?

Why should the evil one have the victory when those in Africa are still waiting to hear the Word of Life?

We knelt to pray about it, and as we waited in His presence the answer came. "My thoughts are not your thoughts, neither are my ways your ways. . . . For as the heavens are higher than the earth, so are my ways higher than your ways, and my thoughts higher than your thoughts" (Isaiah 55. 9). So this turning homeward was not defeat. It only meant that God had a different plan for us. We were comforted, and I could now say with Paul,

"Forgetting the things which are behind, and stretching forward to the things that are before, I press on toward the goal." The Lord would yet lead us into paths of service.

This He did much sooner than I had expected, for we were to find a mission field on the boat that was to carry us home.

Passage had been arranged for us by the American consul. We knew but little about it. The boat was one on a Portuguese line. It was clean and white. The decks were teeming with people. We deposited our luggage quickly in the cabin and returned to the deck to get a last look at beautiful Lisbon harbor. The white buildings with red-tiled roofs made a pleasant picture under the warm June sun. The waterfront below is one of the busiest in all Europe. Boats from Sweden, America, and Spain had dropped anchor there. Not for long did I interest myself in the landscape, for, beautiful though it was, people are the crown of God's creation. I turned to see them. They were well-dressed people with interesting, intelligent faces. I liked them. Their manners were charming, almost courtly. Their emotions were unrestrained. Tears flowed freely as they bade good-by to the loved ones on the shore. I wondered about them.

Who were they? Why was the parting so difficult? Why don't the visitors get off? Can't they see we are beginning to move?

But they were not getting off! They were all passengers bound for America. What a crowd! Seven hundred where three hundred should have been! We were soon to grow so fond of them that we all agreed, "There's not one too many." They were Jewish refugees who had broken all ties with the past and had set their faces toward America. Unhappy faces they were. Deep sorrow was written there. My heart grew light. Here was the mission field I had asked the Lord to lead me to. Oh, it was not a field white unto harvest, but certainly one fertile for the sowing.

I resolved to serve Jesus among them, to live for Him and to speak of Him.

Then the evil one spoke, "They will resent attention from a Gentile. You will antagonize them if you speak your Saviour's name. Presenting the gospel to the Jews is a very specialized service; only those who have studied the psychology of the Hebrew would dare approach them. You can not do this."

It is so the devil works.

But it is Jesus who said, "Will ye hide your light under a bushel?" "All day long have I held out my hands to a disobedient and gainsaying people."

They needed Jesus! They must hear His loving invitation, "Come unto me." I would confess Him.

At first our only service was to *be* the epistle written in flesh and blood. How they blossomed to sincere love and kindly interest. They are not so different from others after all. One dear little black-eyed Jewess accepted a small attention in almost breathless surprise, and expressed her appreciation, saying, "Oh, it's so good to be treated like a human being again." I'm sure it was. Dogs even know better treatment.

The evening meal was pleasant. I do not know what we ate, but we were getting acquainted with our people. We commented upon them as they entered the dining room.

"Here is Rachael."

The one in blue is Rachael.

"The thin little fellow with the eager eyes is Benjamin."

And at the table beyond sat a venerable old man with a long beard. He was Isaac.

I loved them all. They were His own.

1) Mrs. C. Einar Norberg, Miss Esther Olson, Mrs. V. Eugene Johnson, and Miss Velura Kinnan at Sintra, Portugal. (2) Mrs. Johnson at the castle in Sintra, Portugal. (3) Arrival at Maria Kristina Hotel, San Sebastain, Spain. Photos by V. Eugene Johnson.

(1) Unmarried women embarking from Lisbon on Portuguese ship *Mouzinho*, June 10, 1941.
(2) All aboard for Lisbon and America from Sintra, Portugal. Photos by V. Eugene Johnson.

The days that followed were busy days. One hundred and sixteen of the passengers were little children. Their fathers were either in concentration camps or had died there. They were being transported to America to be parcelled out to relatives, to institutions, or to homes which desired them. The woman who had them in charge was an efficient little Russian Jewess, who had just secured her master's degree from Paris. We asked her if we might help her. In rather broken English she replied, "Oh, will you help? The children want to learn 'The Star Spangled Banner,' and then it would be fine if you would help them with their English." Of course we would help! The hour for the meeting was set. There were no late comers. When we reached the salon, these little would-be Americans had packed the place. When Miss Olson sat down at the piano, they cheered enthusiastically. They liked good music and listened with pleasure as Esther struck the majestic chords of our national anthem. They began to struggle with the difficult words. But Jews have a will to work. They copied the words. They worked between rehearsals. They wanted to be good Americans in this "land of the free and home of the brave." Then came the English classes. Their manners were pleasing, and their eagerness to learn made them interesting pupils. But we wanted to tell them of Jesus. They would learn "The Star Spangled Banner" once they reached our shores. There would be many who would teach them to speak English, but who would tell them of Jesus? We longed to claim them for Him.

On the following day we asked the Madam, "May we tell the children of our Saviour." She consented readily, but said, "They won't understand enough English for that." With many of them that was true, but then we took them by guile. I called a missionary friend who told the story very simply in German. We were overjoyed at their response. These children have been so neglected that they have not been taught to hate Jesus or to close their hearts to the gospel. I repeat, it was "a field fertile for the sowing."

But it was not always to be so easy. Their traditional religion had failed to satisfy. Many were skeptics.

One day the testimony was made to a newspaper correspondent and his wife. They listened patiently and kindly, but replied, "Yes, but we are not religious people."

One day Miss Olson spoke to a class of adults. The discussion concerned American money. She pointed out the inscription, "In God We Trust," and then spoke of her faith "built on nothing less than Jesus' blood and righteousness." After class a brilliant doctor, an exile from Paris, approached her saying, "I admire your zeal for your religion, but for myself I want none of it. When I reach America, I only ask that I may have a strong body, a clear mind, and a good job."

Esther told him she hoped he might have all these good gifts in America, and then in a simple, clear way told him how he might possess "The Pearl of Great Price," too. But the prince of this world had closed his heart, and like the rich, young ruler he went sadly away. Pray for him.

One afternoon a young Jew showed us the tickets he must present in order to buy food. They were small, yellow tickets, each marked with a red J to indicate that the customer was Jewish. He explained that Jews could make purchases only between the hours of four and five o'clock in the afternoon. Should he enter a minute before the hour or stay a minute afterward, he was subject to punishment. Fresh fruits, fresh vegetables, milk, chocolates, and sweets were never sold to persons whose tickets bore the red J. Many were the hardships inflicted by this ordinance. There were no Kosher markets, and many of the most orthodox Jews had not eaten meat for five or six years.

I had often been fascinated by a dark-skinned young Jewess. Her features were finely chiseled. She would have been beautiful had it not been for lines of bitterness around her mouth. I wondered what her story might be. One day she told me with pride, "I am an artist." When she saw my interest, she said, "Come, and see my things." Truly she was an artist! God had richly blessed her. She came from a family of artists. Her home held many art treasures. With tears in her eyes she told how young Nazis had entered their home, broken the glass from their windows, and then began to tear the pictures from the wall. When they approached the portrait of her grandmother, she rushed at them and pleaded, "That is a work of art. We can never replace it. It has been in our family for years!"

They were not to be stopped. They destroyed the picture before her eyes, saying, "Why should I save it? It's only an old picture of a Jew."

Little Wolfgang was seven years old. He loved music like the great man for whom he was named. He played selections from the old masters with some ability and much assurance. One day he asked us to meet his mother. She told of taking the child to the dentist in Lisbon. The dentist in fun said to little Wolfgang, "Let me hear how you say 'Heil Hitler.'" Wolfgang stood tall, clicked his heels and said with pride, "I am a Hebrew. Heil Roosevelt!"

When their Sabbath day arrived, I attended their evening service. The rabbi was a serious young man from Luxemburg. The service was long and ritualistic. It seemed a tiresome service to even the most devout. I was amazed at how few attended. The salon was not large, yet there was room to spare. We respected their day of rest and invited them to attend our morning devotion. To our surprise about twenty-five came inside. Others stood at the windows. I am sure the Jewish women observed with a feeling akin to envy the part our girls took in the devotion. During their service the women stood without the glass door. We had no pastor on our boat, so there could be no liturgy or sermon, but there was a Bible study, a few personal testimonies and much singing of hymns of praise.

We thank God for everyone who came. There was, of course, the language barrier, but they could not but feel that there was *joy* and *hope* and *satisfaction* in the hearts of the believers in Jesus.

One Hebrew said, "Oh, these American girls are always happy. They are always having a good time." A missionary explained, "They are truly happy because they have Jesus in their hearts." How we praise God and give Him all the glory for the one Hebrew woman who invited Jesus into her heart while on this voyage! Faithfully pray for her!

One day at the children's hour we had the children do exercises to the rhythm of the music. It somehow did not go off well and became very funny. The children laughed, and even the serious, anxious faces of their elders broke into smiles and then turned to hearty laughter. Afterward one dear Hebrew mother said, "It's so good you make us laugh. I have not laughed for many years." She believed America would be a good land where they could laugh and be happy and forget the cares of the Old World.

There was much talk of citizenship among the newfound friends. Many were homesick for their native land. They had left loved ones behind. Others looked forward eagerly to America, and spoke hopefully of the time when they would become citizens.

On our second night out a baby boy was born. One of the Jewess women inquired next day, "What nationality do you think the baby will be?" I remembered, "His people were Jews. They were citizens of Germany. He was born on a Portuguese boat and they were sailing to America."

I told her quite honestly, "I did not know what his nationality would be."

She replied eagerly, "Oh, I'm sure his mother would like for him to be an American."

How much they were expecting of America! How eagerly they looked forward to citizenship in our land! How they anticipated the day of our arrival! The decks were lined with dark forms at 3:30 in the morning. They were searching in the dusk for the first lights of New York City. My heart yearned over them as I looked upon their expectant faces. I knew so well how soon American citizenship, good though that is, would fail to completely satisfy. Oh, that they might know that citizenship which is in heaven where Jesus is King and where peace is real and is eternal! Oh, that they might know liberty in Christ Jesus and claim the abundant life He came to bring! But how shall they hear without a teacher?

Now the dim shadows of New York's magnificent skyline came into full view. It was time to say good-by. It was hard to leave these dear children of Israel. They are strangers in a strange land. They are as sheep having no shepherd.

Oh, Augustana Synod, let us pray for the peace of Jerusalem and so experience the truth of His promise, "They shall prosper that bless thee." Let us work in the field that has been thrust into our very midst. It means something, does it not, when a Jewish woman will put her arms about a Gentile girl and say, "Pray for my husband"? Oh, let us not be idle while the enemy sows the tares! Let us work while it is day. Night cometh when no man can work.

In company with this party of refugees we began to disembark. Was it not good to be home? It truly gladdened our hearts to know that so soon we should see those whom we love, those who had spent anxious hours in our behalf.

We were anxious that they should see us and be assured that the Lord had truly kept watch above His own.

But stronger in my heart was the feeling of disappointment at not reaching Africa. Yet we know "He doeth all things well." His ways are past tracing out. We know, too, that though the way to Africa is closed, the way to the mercy seat is ever open. We ask that the Lord may keep us faithful in prayer for this field so dear to our hearts, knowing that "more things are wrought by prayer than this world dreams of." Let us pray from the depths of our hearts, "Thy kingdom come!"

HOME AGAIN

Our soul is escaped as a bird out of the snare of the fowlers:
The snare is broken, and we are escaped.
Psalm 124. 7.

After shelling and shipwreck, and weeks on prison ship, and other long days in France and Portugal, the day at last came when the outline of lower New York's skyscrapers met their eyes. Again their eyes looked upon the Statue of Liberty, a gift from a proud land which has lost its liberty and where they but recently had been prisoners of war.

How did it feel to be safely home again?

We shall let the missionaries tell us something about their impressions at being "home again."

MISS ESTHER OLSON

We reached New York on the *S. S. Mouzinho*, Saturday, June 21. Pastor Swanson had come all the way from Minneapolis to meet us. How good it was to see him! And he gave us money, gifts from our good friends in the Augustana Synod who love the Lord Jesus and His cause of missions. We bought clothes and other necessities. We are so grateful to all for this token of love.

The Bethlehem Church in Brooklyn had arranged a farewell service for us in March, and now in less than four months they had a lovely "Welcome Home" for us. The next noon, Wednesday, June 25, we arrived in Jamestown. So many were at the station to meet us. As they sang "Praise God from whom all blessings flow," our hearts thanked Him again.

The good ladies at First Lutheran had prepared a bountiful chicken dinner and we did enjoy it so much. That evening the First Lutheran Church was filled with friends who had cared and now rejoiced.

We had to leave early the next morning for Chicago, and from the time we reached there until we left, the members of the Austin Messiah congregation outdid themselves to welcome us. At the church that evening the choir sang "Thanks Be to God," and the whole service was just that, a great thanksgiving feast to our God and Father.

On Friday evening, Dr. P. O. Bersell and a crowded church greeted us at Messiah in Minneapolis. When we realized what the disaster had meant to him and Pastor Swanson and our Foreign Mission Board, we could only thank God again for bringing us, "Nineteen," safely home.

On Sunday evening the Gustavus Adolphus Church in St. Paul welcomed us. The choir sang "Praise to the Lord, the Almighty, the King of Creation," and truly we can do nothing else. We can praise and adore Him, even if we did not reach Africa. Some day we will understand the why of all. Let us be busy now in praying that this experience may "fall out to the furtherance of the gospel" and that we of the Augustana Synod may pray as we have never done before that the "Amen may sound from His people again," the countless numbers over all the world who will hear the gospel and adore the Lord of lords and King of kings!

DR. C. EINAR NORBERG

A feeling of infinite hope and security was unmistakably evident in the facial expression of most of the passengers on the *Serpa Pinto* as we drew near to the Ambrose Lightship outside New York harbor. One of the refugees, a young professor of economics, said as he beheld the peaceful shore line: "You Americans are simply returning home to that which is commonplace and really belongs to you, but to us this means a new life of hope and freedom, which we have not known for years and had very nearly despaired of ever experiencing again."

After spending a beautiful Sunday on this Portuguese ship in New York harbor we were indeed happy and ready to land on Monday morning. A person can not escape noticing the many contrasts this country presents to almost any other country in the world, even in normal times. How much more apparent it was to us at this unexpected return to America. The experiences we so recently had had on the sea, on the German prison ship, and in the parts of Europe which we saw on our way back, made us more perceptive of the numerous blessings we enjoy in this country. Fear and bitter disappointment, brought on by the horrors of war, are stamped on the countenances of the people in most places where they have had direct contact with the war. Even children bear a stamp of seriousness about them which could only be produced by a chronic calamity.

We had not been in America long before we experienced the truth of the words spoken by the professor of economics on the *Serpa Pinto.* We had come home to friends and relatives. Dr. S. Hjalmar Swanson was at the pier to meet us. He had arranged for several meetings where we could witness of God's protecting care over us, beginning at Brooklyn, and stopping over at Jamestown and Chicago on our way back to Minneapolis. St. Paul, Duluth, Eau Claire, Center City, and many other places were visited later. Everywhere we met many friends and supporters of our mission work.

We were keenly disappointed in our failure to reach Africa. God permitted this sidetracking for some good reason. He took Moses out into the desert for a period of forty years after Moses had taken it into his own hands to right the wrongs suffered by the Israelites. We pray that we may by our experience learn patience and a willingness to submit to God's wisdom.

MRS. C. EINAR NORBERG

It was about 10 P.M. March 20. We were standing on the deck of the *S. S. Zamzam*, watching the clearly illuminated Statue of Liberty and the fantastic lights of Manhattan fade out of view. We were on our way back to Africa. We would not again see these home shores for at least five years.

But here we are back home again! We reached the home waters Sunday, June 22. How good it seemed to see the "land of the free" once more! We had seen some of the pathos and subjection of the Frenchmen, the penury of the Spanish, and had felt the sternness of the Nazi grip.

A group of eight *Zamzam* survivor families were on the *S. S. Serpa Pinto*. All had started out for Africa with full equipment and supplies to last them four to five years. Yes, we were happy to be home, but nevertheless a bit stunned and bewildered over our shattered hopes. Our plans to return to Africa had at first prospered and grown. Just as these plans were about to mature, they were cut down. We had not reached our old homes in Africa.

God sees not only yesterday and today, but also the tomorrow. He never makes a mistake. Our plans can not take precedence over God's plan. We must let each pruning help us grow a little sweeter, a little more tender.

It did seem so good to see Rev. S. Hjalmar Swanson waiting to greet us. His words of welcome were of true cheer. Dr. Emery Ross, secretary of the Foreign Missions Conference of North America, together with his wife, was also there.

The New York Lutheran Home for Women was again thrown open to us. It was the first sense of home feeling we had had since we bade good-by to the kind friends there March 19.

A package of letters was handed us, letters of "welcome home," and full of praises to God for our deliverance. There were letters from Mother and from each of the brothers and sisters, and from other relatives and friends. What an anxious day May 19 had been for them all! Again, we paused to thank God for answered prayers. A prayer often heard among us at our prayer meetings on the prison ship was that God somehow might make our friends and loved ones at home have the comforting assurance that we were alive and well. How wonderfully God answers prayer. We had been on the prison ship thirty-two days before the folks at home even heard of our disaster. May 19 we were sailing along the uneven coastline of Spain, winding our way to St. Jean-de-Luz in occupied France, ready to land.

Relatives and friends have been so very kind to us. We have been touched by their deep concern over our welfare. Above all others, the Friend of all friends is constantly with us.

"Child of My love, fear not the unknown morrow,
Dread not the new demand life make of thee;
Thy ignorance doth hold no cause for sorrow
Since what thou knowest not is known to Me.

"One step thou seest, then go forward boldly,
One step is far enough for faith to see;
Take that, and thy next duty shall be told thee,
For step by step the Lord is leading thee."

FRANK J. EXLEY, D.D.
(From "Step by Step.")

MRS. V. EUGENE JOHNSON

The *S. S. Serpa Pinto*, a Portuguese liner on which we crossed the Atlantic from Lisbon to New York, pulled slowly into Staten Island. We had been awake several hours before we saw the magnificent lights of our great metropolis. A song of thanksgiving to our faithful Lord welled up in our hearts for many journeying mercies. We avoided press photographers and reporters, and hurried to the gangplank, for the long delay in docking had wearied us.

There were deep regrets, too. We had hoped to land in Africa. But since permission to reach Tanganyika Territory had been denied us, we thanked God for bringing us to our free America. Rev. S. Hjalmar Swanson, our warm-hearted executive director, met us at the pier. His smile of welcome and his news about our children and other dear ones whom we had left in America cheered our hearts. He sensed our keen disappointment in failing to reach our needy mission field, but he assured us that God was using our misfortune to arouse the churches in both Africa and America.

When we arrived at the Lutheran Home for Women, faithful friends gave us another warm welcome. Christ seems to dwell there in a special sense which even the little children noticed. We praise God for this Christian home. After purchasing some clothes, we were not so self-conscious about appearing in public.

The same kind friends who had bade us farewell in March gave a reception for us in the Bethlehem Church, Dr. Gideon Olson, pastor, in Brooklyn. We marvelled that such busy people, with a vast mission field at their door, could take time to minister to needy pilgrims.

After the service we boarded the train for Jamestown. Though our little four-year-old was sleepy, he made friends with the congenial conductor, and asked, "Mr. Captain, do you sleep on the top deck, too?"

Many friends had gathered at the station in Jamestown to greet us. The other passengers were deeply impressed by the greeting song which our friends sang for us as we descended from the train. Willing hands had prepared a feast for us in the parlors of the First Church, Jamestown, Rev. Constant Johnson, pastor. In the evening another large, thankful crowd filled the church and gave thanks unto God for the mighty works He has wrought in Africa and other mission fields. It seems more fitting to praise Him for freeing captives bound in sin, for bringing sight to those both physically and spiritually blind, than for delivering us from the enemies which rose up against us.

Upon reaching Chicago, the next evening, we were privileged to gather again in the Messiah Church, Austin, Rev. T. L. Rydback, pastor. The enthusiasm for the extension of God's kingdom was even higher than the weather thermometer. We thank God for the representatives from this congregation who are carrying the glad tidings of salvation to the uttermost parts of the earth.

We were unprepared for the royal welcome back to our home city, Minneapolis, Minn. Our daughter Doris, and our son Daniel, were residing in the city of our birth. You can imagine how our hearts thrilled to see our children, as well as brothers, sisters, nephews, nieces, Grandma Johnson, pastors, and other friends at the depot to meet us. Our dear Messiah Church opened its doors to us, and friends from far and near gathered to hear the welcome greetings from Dr. P. O. Bersell, president of the Augustana Synod; Mrs. Daniel Martin, president of the Synodical Woman's Missionary Society; Dr. Leonard Kendall, pastor of our own Messiah Church, and our simple testimonies.

Rev. C. Vernon Swenson, pastor of Gustavus Adolphus Church, St. Paul, and the Woman's Missionary Society members of the St. Paul District feted us again Sunday evening, June 29. Friends from Oregon and California were present to thank God for answered prayers. We believe that God who makes all things work together for good to those who love Him has made the sinking of the *Zamzam* work for the salvation of souls and the extension of His kingdom.

MRS. ELMER R. DANIELSON

I do not believe any one word has sounded more wonderful to any group of wanderers than that one word "home" to us nineteen after sailing the Atlantic for two months, traveling in Europe, and then crossing the Atlantic again. What a joy this time to see the Statue of Liberty and the skyline of New York, as on June 24 the *S. S. Exeter* brought us again to the shores of our homeland, the shores we had left just three months before. For many of our fellow passengers there was the "welcome home" from the wife or children at the pier, for others it was the parents, sisters or brothers, or even grandparents. That crowd at the pier plainly bore evidence that many were again receiving their loved ones as from the dead. We were so happy to see Rev. Swanson from our Mission Board there to greet us. A brother-in-law was also there.

No sooner had the *S. S. Exeter* docked than we were spotted by radio men, newspaper reporters, and news photographers, all trying to get a real news story. We were eager to get off, and the children did not enjoy these interruptions. From experience, too, we knew that try as hard as you may to tell the story correctly, the printed report is never like the oral. How we would rather just have slipped into oblivion, and yet here was a wonderful opportunity to testify of God's saving grace, His deliverance which was nothing short of miraculous, and His love and care for us all! God alone hath delivered us, and His be all the praise and glory. Without His intervention our lives would long since have been among the "unsung dead."

We did not need to reach the homes of friends and loved ones before we realized what anxiety and concern had been theirs. Beneath it all, we read God's providence, care, love, guidance, and His plans in all things. How we rejoiced for the many prayers God answered in the care of our loved ones those days! It was interesting to hear how the news had been received by communities less affected as to relationship, but women gathering in the backyards weeping and talking of the *Zamzam*, and praying in their hearts, was no doubt quite a general picture. In schoolrooms some teachers said it was like a funeral that first day, little classmates would not be comforted that all would be well. The best news was of the prayer services called in our behalf at different churches, and loved ones interceding as they worked. It seemed that with the gloom there was still a ray of hope with most of them. How I rejoiced that the hours of suspense were less than two days! In my own case, it required much grace from God to *just wait* until my husband's letters started arriving from Africa to learn what he had actually passed through. I knew it would be a real ordeal for him. I had received a cable, yes, two, in Sintra, so I knew that all was well, and I thank God that He saw him safely through, that as *his* day was, just so God had supplied the strength to meet that day's trials.

Home again! What a relief just to unpack suitcases, and not be packing and unpacking again for a season. I did not reach my goal, Africa, and coming back here is not coming "home" in the true sense of the word so long as "our daddy" is not here, but both he and I feel so rich in that God saved the jewels for us. I can not be *disappointed* in *God's appointments* for me and mine. Someday we'll read the "why's and wherefore's" of this last experience. Until then we just abide in His will, knowing that Jesus doeth all things well.

The greatest gratification through it all has come when friends have told us they have been blest spiritually through seeing God's hand in it all. A big shower of beautiful letters from new friends in the Lord has come, letters praising only *faith, fortitude,* and what God hath done. I would like to share a poem a friend sent me the other day which really expresses my innermost feelings now at home. May it truly be said of us that we were "saved to serve."

Traveling with God

My plans were made, I thought my path all bright and clear,
My heart with song o'erflowed, the world seemed full of of cheer.
My Lord I wish to serve, to take Him for my guide,
To keep so close that I could feel Him by my side,
And so I traveled on.

But suddenly, in skies so clear and full of light,
The clouds fell thick and fast, the days seemed changed to night;
Instead of paths so clear and full of things so sweet,
Rough things and thorns and stones seemed all about my feet.
I scarce could travel on.

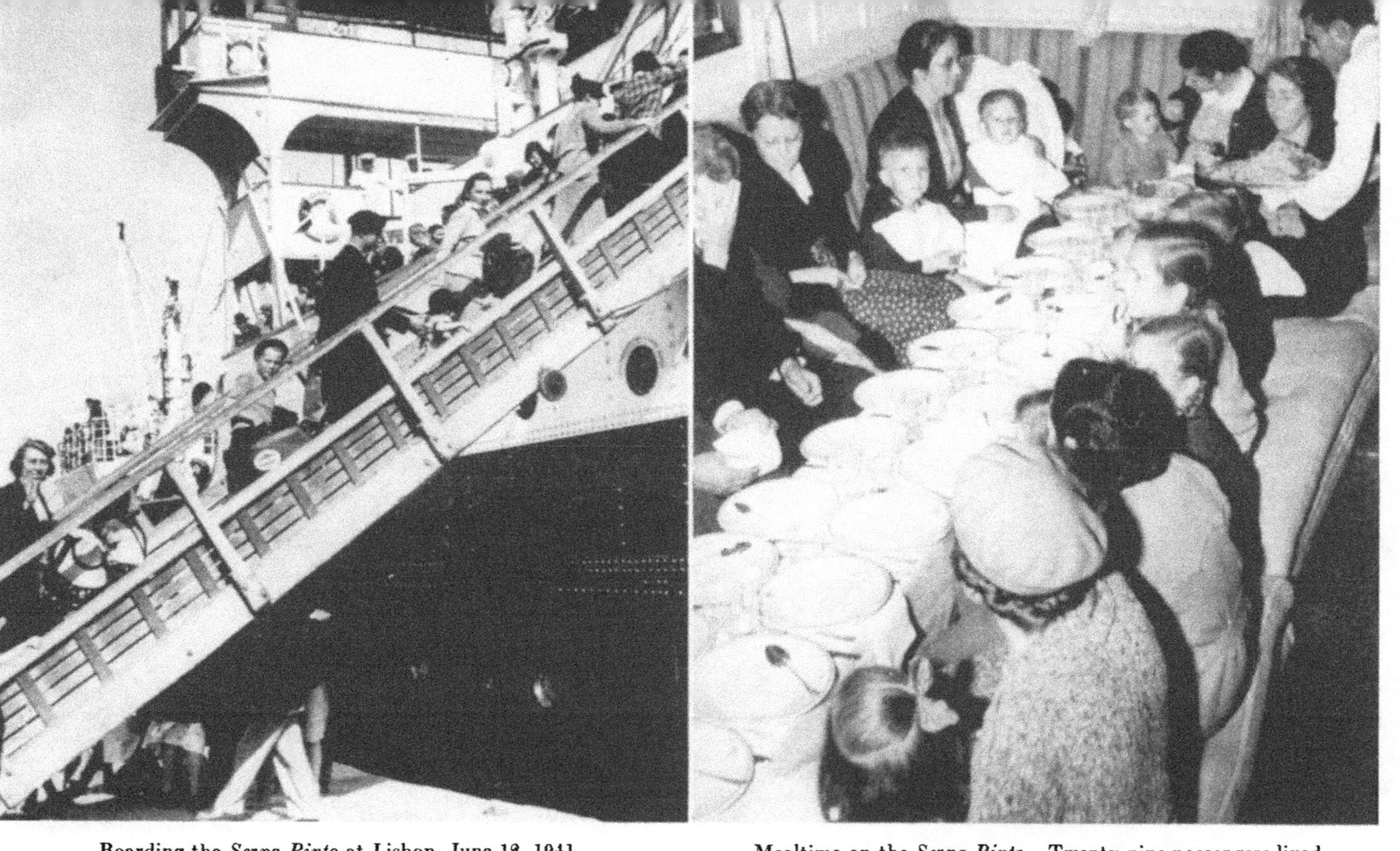

Boarding the *Serpa Pinto* at Lisbon, June 12, 1941.
Photos by V. Eugene Johnson.

Mealtime on the *Serpa Pinto.* Twenty-nine passengers lived, ate, and slept in this room (16x24) for eleven days.

I bowed my head and wondered why this change should
come,
And murmured, "Lord, is this because of aught I've done?
Has not the past been full enough of pain and care?
Why should my path again be changed to dark from fair?"
But still I traveled on.

I listened, quiet and still; there came a voice,
"This path is mine, not thine. I made the choice.
Dear child, this service will be best for thee and me,
If thou wilt simply trust and leave the end to me."
And so we travel on.

—J. J. M.

REV. RALPH D. HULT

Monday morning, June 30, the *S. S. Excalibur* reached the outer New York Harbor after a good voyage from Lisbon. There was a heavy fog that morning, so we were obliged to move very slowly as we entered the inner harbor after taking on our pilot. Many Americans, who had been away from home for a long time, were lined up on the port side of the ship, hoping to get a glimpse of the Statue of Liberty. A large number of refugees from war-torn Europe, coming to America for the first time, were also in the group on that side of the ship's deck. "There she is!" We beheld her, veiled in the morning mist, and it seemed that we could almost hear her speak a word of welcome. Thank God, we were home again!

No sooner had our ship reached its berth, than a group of newspaper men came aboard. Rev. and Mrs. Williams and I, the last remnant of the *Zamzam* missionary group, were surprised to find ourselves cornered, pictured and questioned. We had thought that by now the story of the *Zamzam* was too old to be news. In the customs' shed I was pleasantly surprised to see Mr. Karl Slotte, of the New York Lutheran Home for Women. He brought me to the Home, where I found letters from my loved ones, the first word of any kind from them to reach me in nearly three months. How good it was to sit down there in the peace and privacy of our Lutheran Home to read letters from wife and children, from parents, brothers, sisters, and friends! The friends in the Home did everything in their power to make me comfortable, as they also did when we were passing through New York City last March to leave for Africa. Mother Evald spared no effort to anticipate our every need.

At the first opportunity I called at the Lutheran Church House, where the Lutheran World Action has its office. Here awaited a very pleasant surprise. Immediately upon entering the office, Doctor Long read to me a letter just received from the director of the Leipzig Missionary Society of Germany. The director was informing the Lutheran World Action office of the reaction of missionary circles in Germany to the news of what had happened to the missionaries on the *Zamzam.* He stated that a representative of the missionary societies in Germany had pleaded with the Nazi government for our speedy release, so that we might continue on our way to Africa. This was good news, indeed.

"Blest be the tie that binds
Our hearts in Christian love.
Our fears, our hopes, our aims are one,
Our comforts and our cares."

It is needless to state that I took the first westbound train available after the interviews at the Lutheran Church House in New York City. A message brought me the good news that my dear wife would meet me at her parental home in Illinois. I was deeply grateful to God for His care for us, as I saw my wife and three of the children at the station in Moline. After a brief visit with relatives, we started for our humble home in the Ozarks, where the other seven of our family were awaiting us. After an all-night drive we arrived at Springfield, Mo., early in the morning of Sunday, July 6.

Here I must draw the curtain. The memories of that morning I can not write about. United as a family once more about the family altar, our hearts sang praises to God, from whom all blessings flow. The Lord, our keeper, had preserved us from all evil. He had preserved my going out and my coming in.

HOW THE NEWS CAME TO AFRICA

And many of the Jews had come to Martha and Mary, to console them. John 11. 19.

When the crushing news came to us here in America that the *S. S. Zamzam* was lost with all its passengers, we naturally thought of our missionaries in Africa, especially Pastors Danielson and Olson. Had they heard about it, too, and just how much had they heard? How long was their time of suspense?

Apparently their experiences were similar to ours. Their thoughts naturally turned to the fellow worker, who, as it then seemed, had suffered the most tragic loss. Natives as well as missionaries endeavored to be of comfort. We count it a privilege to share some of the correspondence which came to Pastor Elmer R. Danielson.

Kinampanda Training School
May 19, 1941

Dear Elmer:

Many thanks for your kind letter received this afternoon and for your sympathies in this hour of bereavement.* But what are my sorrows compared to your overwhelming sorrow now? We can not find words to express our own sorrow, too, at the probable loss of that precious cargo on the *Zamzam*.

We heard the news over the radio just by chance this evening, and we were just paralyzed and so overcome we did not know what to do. Miss Lindbeck and three of the teachers happened to be present, and we could only bow our heads before our heavenly Father who knows best, and commit to Him you who have been bereft and the others who have perhaps gone on before. Alice and I share with you with bleeding hearts this overwhelming sorrow, and may God in His mercy strengthen you as never before, and comfort you as none of us can.

Yet, there need not be all hope lost, since the news, though quite detailed, held out hope by its indefiniteness. It is not known definitely whether it was a submarine or a raider. In fact it was mentioned that some were rescued and on board a German raider, sixty Americans altogether, so it was stated. Even if many lost their lives, God in His mercy may have spared your loved ones and you may yet see them here in this world.

May our Saviour enfold you in His arms and fill your soul with comfort and peace in this very dark hour. Let us also remember the thousands who have suffered in this war, women and children, in London, Belgrade, and many other places.

Yours in deepest sympathy,

MILAN
(Milan Lany)

* Mr. Lany had recently lost his father.

SINGIDA MISSION STATION
May 20, 1941

Commit thy ways unto the Lord:
Trust also in him, and he will bring it to pass. Psalm 37. 5.

DEAR BROTHER DANIELSON:

That "It," which the Lord our God has permitted to come to pass, and which He still is permitting to continue, is covered with deep and heavy clouds, so that our eye can not see, and we are forced to "walk by faith and not by sight." But we know that beyond that heavy cloud, there is also the proof and manifestation of His great love.

You, dear brother, more than any one of us, must be shocked and deeply burdened, but we also know that you will be specially favored by our dear Saviour's help and strength in this time of need.

"In pastures green," not always, sometimes He
Who knoweth best, in kindness leadeth me,
In weary ways, where shadows be.

Only for this: I know He holds my hand;
So, whether led in green or desert land,
I trust, although I may not understand.

And more than this: where'er the pathway lead,
He gives to me no helpless, broken reed,
But His own hand, sufficient for my need.

So, where He leads me I can safely go:
And in the blest hereafter I shall know
Why in His wisdom He hath led me so.

It was an awful shock to hear that terrible bit of news last night. My radio was not working any too well, and we were just listening casually, when the words "*Steamship Zamzam*" struck our ears. Well, we stayed up most of the night trying to find more on the radio, hoping for more news from American stations, but we could not get anything more.

We know that the precious human cargo aboard that ill-fated vessel was in God's good hands, and "His hand is not shortened" that He can not still do miracles. We wait and pray for such a miracle of His love.

I feel optimistic that all is well and that in God's good time we shall receive the good news. But our sincere sympathy goes out to you, especially during these burdensome days of waiting, for there is nothing quite so hard to bear as uncertainty.

Our prayers will go up to the throne of grace. Jesus Christ, our Saviour, will hear, and He will "not leave us, nor forsake us." His grace is sufficient for all our needs.

In sincere love and sympathy, my wife and daughter join me.

Jesus will be very close to you at this time.

Your fellow workers in Jesus' name and service,

A. C. ZEILINGER

(*Translated*)

May 20, 1941

To Dear Pastor E. R. Danielson

DEAR MASTER:

I have much sorrow to hear the bad news about the missionaries, what happened to the ship they were on. I have heard through Mama Engelmann today in the church at the ninth hour (3 P.M.). That same hour (immediately) I went out from the church to come to you, to see you, but Mama told me I should not go, and that is why I write this letter, that it may be the same as if I were with you in your sorrow, in this great trouble.

1. I thought very much, but I have not knowledge (do not understand).

2. I have looked very much, but I can not see.

3. I know one thing only.

4. I see one thing only.

5. That one thing is: God only, *He knows.*

6. God only, *He sees.*

I pray my God and your God, our God and their God, that He may supply all your needs in this matter, that He may comfort you in this great sorrow.

May God give strength in this your trouble, Bwana (dear Master).

TEACHER YESAYA ARONI

(*Translated*)

KIOMBOI MISSION

For Rev. E. R. Danielson

REVEREND:

Greetings many because of the love of our Lord Saviour.

Master, I have fears and I have doubts because I have received news that Mama and the children are not in this world now. Now I want to know if it is true that they are not in the world now. I loved Mama. I wish that we may see them living, Mama and the children. It is not true, is it? Mama and the children, have they left this world?

I have been sick these days, pains and sores in my feet. I can not walk much and that is why I do not get much news or many words (reports). Just so Mama and the children are well!

I greet you very much. I would like very much to see you, but I am a little ill (i.e., can not come). God will help because of His love.

I am your former cook, Msengi Kitundu.

NAGUNIKA KITUNDU

Kiomboi Mission Station.

WEMBERE MISSION,
P. O. KINYANGIRI, TANGANYIKA
May 20, 1941

American Consul
Nairobi, Kenya

DEAR SIR:

Forgive the unsteadiness of this letter.

After being up all night with a young Scotch miner in delirium from blackwater fever, the news was broken to me in the morning that the radio last night and this morning reported that the *S. S. Zamzam* had been sunk by enemy action.

On that ship were my wife and six children. Friend, the blow is too great. I can not believe that they are gone. On the boat were also Dr. and Mrs. C. E. Norberg and three children, Pastor and Mrs. V. Eugene Johnson and two children, Pastor Hult, who left his wife and children in the States (as I did last year in face of the Italian threat), Miss Esther Olson and Miss Velura Kinnan, teachers on their first assignment to Africa. There was a large number of American missionaries and Red Cross workers on board.

What can be done to find out for certain what happened? Are they on a raider? Were they all lost? This is too much for me to believe. Will the State Department press for news with undiminishing vigor, and let me know every result?

It is impossible for me to face you with all that is surging through me, but it won't take much imagination for you to understand that I am about broken to pieces, as I see helpless, innocent little kiddies, and the bravest little mother and wife on earth, going through hell's ordeal, and I, the husband and daddy, not there to help them.

Every tiny bit of help and information you can get for me to solve this just too overwhelming tragedy will be appreciated beyond all measure in words.

Ironically, some of these workers were coming to help supervise the tremendous mission fields of the German societies, which are now under our superintendence for the duration of the war.

Respectfully yours,
E. R. DANIELSON

RURUMA MISSION STATION
May 23, 1941

DEAR FELLOW WORKERS:

Yes, what a shock to be listening rather complacently to the radio and then hear right out of a clear sky the tragic news of the sinking of the *Zamzam!* How our hearts and prayers were united in our little mission group, and not least for Pastor Danielson. No one can imagine how difficult it has been for him these days. Dr. Moris and I had planned to break the news to him in person. He had, however, spent that night in the care of a young miner at Msigiri, suffering with blackwater fever (subsequently he died), and Dr. Moris broke the news to him there at Msigiri. It was almost more than he could stand. And so a tremendous load has been lifted from him and us all as the reassuring news has come over that same ether that they are safe, and still with us in the land of the living. Our "Kyrie eleison" has been changed to "Te Deums" and "Alleluias." We have been reminded of the word in Hebrews of receiving our own again from the dead. Blessed be the name of the Lord! Let us keep on praying until we shall see our beloved coworkers with us here face to face. That will be a "siku kuu"!

A telegram was immediately dispatched to the Agency, *S. S. Zamzam*, Capetown, after receipt of the first news of the ship's sinking. A reply may come in the post this week end. By request a cable will be sent to the Board unless something comes from them with this post (i.e., a cable). There is not much we can do but wait and pray. We hope we may get more definite news soon. May the Lord deal kindly with them!

May the Lord continue to guide us with His counsel, and give us grace and wisdom to know and to do His will!

Faithfully yours,
GEO. N. ANDERSON

RURUMA
May 24, 1941

DEAR PASTOR DANIELSON:

I rejoice with you over the reassuring news that your loved ones and the other missionaries are safe. We humbly unite our feeble thanksgivings with yours. May the Lord continue to keep His merciful and blessed hands protectingly over them all.

I am sorry that we did not catch over the radio the name of the place where they were landed. Is it possibly the French islands south of Capetown? The *Standard* received tomorrow will probably give the name. They must be unable to cable or it seems we would have heard from them. There may be further news in the post tomorrow. Shall cable the Board as you desire, if nothing comes tomorrow. Just how should it be worded?

Sincerely,
GEO. N. ANDERSON

SUNDAY, MAY 25, 1941

DEAR DANIELSON:

I've wanted to write or to see you so badly these days, but words seem so futile. Our hearts and souls reach out to Him who knows all. Also we know He is the ever-present One. All things work together for good.

We have been fortunate in getting American news here. This A.M. says they might be released this week. I certainly feel that all are well. We know that you would like to share Lillian's work and responsibilities, but thanks be to God that Esther, Velura, as well as Pastor Hult, were there to help. God loves His little children so very much.

Just this, as carrier is in a hurry.

We pray always.

MARGARET

May 25th

DEAR FRIEND:

I haven't written you before, but not because I have not thought of doing so. Nay, one has felt as if God were, oh, suspending one's soul in prayer for you and for them, and constantly it is so. May God's abiding love, constant through storm and even loss, make all these sobering experiences spiritual exercises for all who are affected. We shall continue to remember them always in a special way until we know for certain they are all taken care of and safe back home or on the way out here. The picture of Lillian and those children has been so vivid in my mind these sore days. What must it be in yours! God continue to bless you with strength to carry on here, faith to calm the anguish within, and trust that they will be cared for though you can not be the one to do it. And just everything you need for just these days.

Please, if you are writing to her in U.S.A., in case they are brought back there, or wherever it may be, tell her that we are thinking of her.

Sincere greetings,
ELEANOR LINDBECK

(*Translated*)

May 26, 1941

FOR MY DEAR MASTER, WHO IS REV. DANIELSON:

Greetings in Jesus Christ our Saviour.

I have had much sorrow these days because I heard that Mama and the children have finished, in the sea. Now I hear that they saved them, and I rejoice in my heart.

I am here in the hospital these days, a little well (improving).

God Himself will guard them in His mercy on their journey.

I am your friend in the Lord,
PAULINA NYINGI

OUT OF THE DEPTHS

ELMER R. DANIELSON

Deep calleth unto deep at the noise of thy waterfalls:
All thy waves and thy billows are gone over me.
Psalm 42. 7.

WEMBERE MISSION STATION
May 22, 1941

On Sunday afternoon, May 19, I was notified by Stan, Dr. Moris, that Mac at Kirondatal Mine had blackwater fever, and was sinking. I had just returned from a visit to a colony of uncared-for lepers. The mail came, but no news from my sweetheart as to where they were. But there was her airmail, saying that Swanson had just informed her (March 12) that her visa could not be gotten. "You must wait." There was mother's letter of March 24, saying she had seen Lillian and the kiddies the night before they embarked. But my anxiety is growing by bounds for tomorrow makes it sixty days since they left New York. Where can they be? They were to tell us when they reached Capetown.

Monday I was in the grip of restless forebodings. I got halfway ready to visit Mtemi Kingo at Shelui, but letters arrived from Ruruma and Kinampanda, requiring immediate answer. I almost went at noon, but it was terrifically hot, and I was not sure if the Chief would still be there. At three a courier brought Stan's note that if I wanted to see Mac I should come now. A case was hastily packed, and I went, arriving there at five. Miss Safemaster, Mrs. Ramsey, and Stan were there, all very tired. Stan had to return to Kiomboi. I stayed awake that night with MacDonald to help him, and to reach his heart a bit, if possible.

But Mac was delirious almost all night. He fitfully slept from three to three-thirty. It was work, physical, mental, spiritual, to keep him in bed. He responded to prayer, but he was not at ease in heart. It was a hard night for all.

The day dawned with sunshine, and the birds sang, but not for poor Mac. We prayed again, to which he quietly responded in a few moments of mental clearness.

It was still early, about seven o'clock, and Stan arrived. Miss Safemaster stepped into the sick man's room, and said Stan wanted to see me outside. Something was not right, my heart told me. Could it be—a fearful thought ran through my mind.

His face was broken in lines and tears, and his voice would hardly work. He had not slept all night. He took me by the arm, and fitfully said: "The *Zamzam* has been reported over last night's radio as long overdue, and it is feared it has been sunk by enemy action."

Who could grasp anything as terrible as all that in a brief moment? Moment by moment the anguish grew until my world was inky black. The bravest mother and sweetheart on earth, precious six little kiddies, innocent, helpless, all gone! My heart broke and cried out to God: "No! No! No! It can't be so! It is too terrible! It is too much!"

Somehow I drove to Kiomboi with Miss Safemaster. She took me to Elveda's home, and on my knees the soul's storm broke. Brave little sweetheart and six little kiddies, all I have on earth, gone? NO! I cried to our Father in anguish, they through hell's ordeal, and I, the daddy and husband, not there even to comfort them with a word or a touch! We, Elveda and I, drove to Ruruma in the daze of a tortured mind and heart to get more exact news. It is too terrible to believe! It is too much!

In anguish unbelievable, something lurked in the deeper recesses of my soul. Maybe it is not true; maybe the ship will come through; maybe they are on a raider; but, then what?

Somehow I could not believe our Father would permit them to be lost, and all in His work here.

But false hopes are dangerous. I want the truth. We came back to Kiomboi, and I wrote a letter to the American Consul at Nairobi to get me the truth.

Bitter, bitter thoughts against WAR! Why people tolerate this hell on earth! War has to go!

If it is true that my precious companion-in-life and precious kiddies, all dedicated to serve God with me, are gone, then I want to go. I do not think He would expect me to stay on alone. I would not be any good.

What hell that sweet woman and innocent kiddies must have gone through. Father, Father, Father! NO! NO! NO! It can not be so! It is too much!

And we have only sought Thy will. We separated, too, for Thy sake, but only for a season, not like this, never.

The Egyptian flag, what is that these days? Germany says the ship carried war materials. Would our State Department have permitted women and children to go on a ship, laden with war materials, which is always liable to be sunk? Who is it that is laying the lives of women and children on the altar of satanic greed?

Oh, why? Oh, why? The heart cries, and dark and bitter and agonized thoughts come and go fitfully.

The ray of hope shines through also, but, oh, how faintly!

I had been awake all night, and now came the first night after the news. What a night to face, except for a ray of light that came over the nine o'clock London broadcast that the American government had sent a note to Berlin asking the whereabouts of the 142 American passengers on the *Zamzam.* The "whereabouts," what does that mean?

With the help of medicine I slept some, but with the break of dawn, the anguish broke again. Visions of little kiddies drowning, being maimed, or killed, starving in little boats, separated from one another, cold, wet, thirsty, frightened, facing death, tortured in spirit and mind and flesh, lost on some forsaken spot, lost so cruelly, tore my heart, and I, their daddy and the husband of that brave, sweet girl and mother, NOT THERE! And we thought we were doing God's will when I came alone last July, leaving one another for Jesus' sake ONLY!

There is a ray of comfort, too, in knowing that fellow passengers would help Lillian and the kiddies with unlimited sacrifice, but I am the one who should have cared for my sweet wife and little kiddies, my own, my own from God. That is the anguish! Norberg and Johnson could be with their loved ones through this hell's ordeal, but mine went through ALONE!

The day of the 21st, Wednesday, arrived. But it was inky black to me. The zinnias outside the window no longer looked alive. The brilliant bougenvillia was also colorless. The sunshine was not true. Nothing was left for me. I might just as well have been a dead treetrunk as far as interest in life was concerned.

Lachman Singh, a Sikh, comes with eyes brimming with tears: "That mama is not dead. That mama and those children are not dead." Desai, another Indian, choked with grief could only say: "Mungu ike, Mungu ike." (God is there, God is there.) Do you call such compassion the compassion of heathen? As the news spread, congregations broke into tears, teachers were at a loss for words, and here, there and everywhere there was no sleep that night. It was a night spent in torn grief and crying to God. The news reached Ushola, as the teachers gathered, and Nehemia peddled fifty miles back and forth from Ushola to Ruruma to find out the truth. He did it in less than half a day, while the teachers waited for his return. Today Petro came thirty-five miles by bike to comfort me and to pray with me. A young African leader, removed from heathendom by less than fifteen years, filled with Christ's compassion and concern for mama, and the children, and me! He comforted me from the gospel, and in beautiful pleading with the Father.

And in the midst of my anguished tears, a still voice said: "There still is hope."

Word came about eight o'clock that MacDonald was sinking. They wanted me and Stan. I did not want to go, but a voice said: "Go!" Can I bury him when my heart is in anguish over my loved ones?

What peculiar circumstances under which to hear such tragic news. Coincidence? No, God guides things. They just don't happen, not matters like this.

Lillian would want me to go to Mac, and my little kiddies would want their daddy to help. I could not sit at Kiomboi all day. I would not be helping either my sweetheart or kiddies or Mac. So I went with all my anguish and torn thoughts and emotions.

Mac was unconscious and breathing hard. Poor boy, only twenty-five, dying, practically through neglect of self. We commit his soul to Thee, O Father, who knoweth him. He responded to prayer. A Bible was found among his books, given to him in 1937 by his pastor, when he first left Scotland for Africa.

But Africa, what do you do to these young, white men from Europe?

There was now a very sweet interlude in the midst of the pressing tragedies here in the bush of Africa. We baptized little Elizabeth Helena, the sweet baby of Mr. and Mrs. Wessels of Kirondatal Gold Mine. What a fine young

Christian couple, clean-living, praying, conscientious, warm with human kindness and gratitude. By her daddy's bedside, sweet Elizabeth received the blessed baptism into her Saviour's life and love. It was a moment of heaven on earth.

We returned to Mac, and fifteen minutes later he passed into eternity.

His room was bare, a picture of mother on the wall, also of a sister, a few books, his clothes and traveling cases, that was all that was left by this young man, who lived in the bush near a tiny gold mine, employing three white men.

We took Mac by car twenty-five miles to Sekenke, the main mine. The grave was hard to dig. Time passed slowly. The body was being prepared in the center room of the Cuthertson house, and I was in a side room, preparing a message. I had already chosen at the first news on Sunday the story of Jesus and the widow's son, showing His compassion for the sorrowing, and His power over death. Was that His message to me, too, today?

The door opened, and Miss Safemaster entered, and joyfully proclaimed, "They're saved! They have been landed on French soil. Mr. Haman will tell you more. He heard it last night over the ten o'clock German broadcast." I stepped into the center room, where MacDonald's body was being prepared for burial, and while Haman and I put on Mac's clothing and shirt, Haman said, yes, the German news last night said the Americans were safe on French soil. So many emotions had spent themselves in me the past thirty-six hours, that I was dull. And could I dance for joy there—at a funeral?

But where are they? French West Africa seemed to me the most likely place. More mental pictures disturbed me, of my wife's mental despair, and relentless tiredness of mind and body, of shortage of food and water, of heat and sickness in some desolate spot. But hope is growing. And I have a funeral to attend to. Hardly ever do these whites hear God's Word, and how I want to speak to them so that they will know Him.

At 7:15 o'clock we had the house service, whites and a few Indians together, gathered around a cross at the foot of the coffin. The service came to an end, and the coffin preceded us to the station car for carriage to the cemetery. As I followed, Mr. Fischer, a Belgian, a director of the Mining Corporation, took a hold of my sleeve, and said: "It is true. It has been confirmed by the Vichy Government that they are safe on French soil. I heard it at six o'clock."

We went to the burial ground, a mile and a half away, and by car and lantern light, surrounded by a sea of white and black and Indian faces, we laid Mac away. Stan and I sang, "I Know That My Redeemer Liveth." A swarthy Jamaican, a gardener, standing by, joined in.

We got back to the Ramsey home, and someone said: "The London news is on. Let's listen. Maybe there is something." The announcer was already speaking, and it was nearing the end, and then it came clearly: "It is confirmed by the Vichy Government that 140 Americans have been landed at St. Jean-de-Luz on the Basque coast."

Joy, peace, yes, but where are the two missing ones, and who are they?

The wonderful hand of God begins to shine through the darkness. Oh, for a word from my beloved, that brave little wife and mother and my God-given kiddies! Grant it, Father, in Thy mercy!

When wilt Thou bring me to them, or them to me, to serve Thee together? Furnish me with the news which is lacking. Give me grace to be patient. Let me taste of the graciousness of uncertainty. Carry my loved ones in Thy arms like a Father. Protect them under Thy wings. They need it, O God.

Strange, on May 19 last year, Lillian and I and the children left Lindsborg for Africa, but had to turn back. On May 19 this year the terrible news of the *Zamzam* came over the air. Today, May 22, is my birthday. What a miraculous, divine present, the news of my beloved's and children's safety.

Father, Father, I thank Thee!

PASSENGERS AND PERSONNEL OF THE "S. S. ZAMZAM"

Captain: W. G. Smith.
Chief Engineer: John Burns.
Chief Officer: Stanko Fiedel.
Doctor: Dr. A. B. Rufail.
Chief Purser: Youssef Farrang.
Crew: 137, chiefly Egyptian (Mohammedan).

Passengers: American, 137; Canadian, 26; British, 15; North Rhodesia, 1; Bahama Islands, 2; Hong Kong, 2; South Africa, 5; Swaziland, 1; Kenya, 2; Belgian, 4; French, 1; Italian, 1; Norwegian, 1.

MISSIONARIES ABOARD THE "ZAMZAM"

Africa Inland Mission:

Dr. and Mrs. H. Barnett, Kenya.
Rev. and Mrs. Roy F. Brill and five children, Kenya.
Miss Jessie Blanchard.
Miss Ruth Burgess, Belgian Congo.
Rev. and Mrs. L. J. Buyse and two children.
Rev. and Mrs. W. Fred Fix and daughter, Tanganyika.
Rev. and Mrs. W. J. Guilding, Kenya.
Miss Harriet M. Halsey, Belgian Congo.
Miss Alice E. Landis, Kenya.
Rev. and Mrs. W. A. Mundy.
Miss Carol O. Turner.
Rev. and Mrs. J. Fred Young.

Assembly of God:

Rev. and Mrs. Paul E. Derr, Tanganyika.
Mr. and Mrs. Claude T. Keck, Tanganyika.

Augustana Synod Lutheran:

Mrs. Elmer R. Danielson and six children, Tanganyika.
Rev. Ralph D. Hult, Tanganyika.
Rev. and Mrs. V. Eugene Johnson and two children, Tanganyika.
Miss Velura Kinnan, Tanganyika.

Dr. and Mrs. C. Einar Norberg and three children, Tanganyika.
Miss Esther M. Olson, Tanganyika.

Baptist, National Convention:

Rev. and Mrs. T. O. Dosum and daughter, Liberia.

Baptist, Northern:

Dr. Dana M. Albaugh, executive secretary of Foreign Mission Board.

Baptist, Mid-Mission:

Florence Almen, French Equatorial Africa.

Baptist, Southern:

Miss Elma Elam, Nigeria.
Miss Isabelle Moore, Nigeria.
Dr. and Mrs. J. Paul O'Neal and daughter, Nigeria.

Brethren of Christ:

Rev. and Mrs. David B. Hall and two children, South Rhodesia.

Church of the Brethren:

Miss Grace Byron, French Equatorial Africa.
Miss Mary A. Engel, West Africa.
Miss Sylvia Oiness, Nigeria.
Miss Ruth Snyder, French Equatorial Africa.
Miss Ruth Utz, Nigeria.
Mr. and Mrs. Robert Williams, French Equatorial Africa.

Congo Inland Mission:

Dr. and Mrs. Merle H. Schwartz, Belgian Congo.

Disciples of Christ:

Mr. and Mrs. W. H. Edwards, Belgian Congo.
Mr. and Mrs. A. G. Henderson, Belgian Congo.

Norwegian Lutheran Church:

Miss Alida Agrimson, Belgian Congo.
Sister Olette Berntsen, Belgian Congo.
Miss Olga Guttormsen, Zululand, South Africa.

Presbyterian, Southern:

Mr. and Mrs. T. K. Morrison and two children, Belgian Congo.
Miss Dora Lena Reynolds, Belgian Congo.
Dr. and Mrs. Tinsley Smith, Jr., and son, Belgian Congo.

Presbyterian, United:

James P. McKnight.
Rev. and Mrs. Paul J. Smith, Sudan.

Progressive Brethren:

Mr. and Mrs. G. C. Morrill and two children, French Equatorial Africa.

S. A. General Convention:

Rev. and Mrs. R. Neilson Muir, Angola.

Scandinavian Alliance:

Mr. and Mrs. Irl McAllister, Swaziland, South Africa.
Miss Lydia Rogalsky, Swaziland, South Africa.

Seventh Day Adventist:

Mrs. H. G. Hankins, South Africa.
Miss Helen M. Hyatt.
Mr. and Mrs. J. S. Russell and daughter.
Mr. and Mrs. T. J. Jenkins.
Mr. and Mrs. Stanley Johnson.

Sudan Interior Mission:

Rev. and Mrs. Walter A. Ohman, Anglo Egyptian Sudan.
Miss Mary S. Beam, Anglo Egyptian Sudan.

World Wide Evangelization Crusade:

Miss Rhodie Olson, Belgian Congo.
Mr. and Mrs. E. V. Steele, Belgian Congo.

Free Methodist:

Rev. and Mrs. Geo. A. Belknap and daughter, Belgian Mandated Territory.
Miss Mary Thompson, Belgian Mandated Territory.
Mae P. Armstrong, Portuguese East Africa.

Roman Catholic:

Rev. Father Robert Barsalou, Basutoland, South Africa.
Rev. Brother Raoul Bergeron.
Rev. Brother Gerard Boulanger.
Rev. Father Hermenegelde Charbonneau.
Rev. Brother Roland Cournoyer.
Rev. Father Bernard Desnoyer.
Rev. Brother Andre Fredette.

Rev. Father Phillippe Goudreau.
Rev. Brother Paul Juneau.
Rev. Father Joseph Laflamme.
Rev. Father L. Larivierre.
Rev. Father Aime Lavallee.
Rev. Brother Antoine Lavallee.
Rev. Brother J. E. Leo.
Rev. Brother Maurice Nadeau.
Rev. Father Gerard Paquet.
Rev. Father Pierre P. Pellerin.

Epilogue

The Zamzam story lives on! Beginning in 1991, fifty years after the Zamzam's sinking, survivors and families have gathered for reunions six times. In a spirit of thanks to God, survivors have shared memories of their unique experience at sea. Newsletters, too, have helped create a close bond among them.

That list of survivors, with their storehouse of memories, has dwindled drastically with the passing of time. By the year 2008 only two of the known twenty-nine living survivors had been adults on the Zamzam. Of course, older child survivors remember the Zamzam episode quite clearly, but many of the children had been too young to remember the Zamzam at all. Reunions have helped make the story their own.

The Zamzam story continues to be shared in a variety of ways, old and new. The story is still told at church and community programs, often accompanied by newspaper articles. Newer media include a website (www.Zamzamship.net), a DVD/video titled *"Zamzam: A Missionary Odyssey"*, and the book, *Miracle at Sea* by Eleanor Anderson (Quiet Waters Publications). The republishing of this 1941 book is another testimony to interest in the Zamzam story.

Zamzam materials are now being preserved at the ELCA Archives in Elk Grove, IL; the Billy Graham Center Archives in Wheaton, IL; and the Joyner Library, East Carolina University, Greenville, NC. Several survivors keep collections, too. For more information, please send an email to eleander@cox.net or www.quietwaterspub.com.

As Zamzam research continues, more is being learned about the Canadian survivors, the internment camps, the German officers and crew, the motives which prompted the sinking, the Egyptian crew and more. Indeed, the story goes on!

"Give thanks to the Lord, because He is good,
and his love is eternal." (Psalm 118:1)

Eleanor Danielson Anderson, May, 2008

www.ingramcontent.com/pod-product-compliance
Lightning Source LLC
Chambersburg PA
CBHW032101080426
42733CB00006B/374

* 9 7 8 1 9 3 1 4 7 5 3 5 8 *